MOULDED AND SLIP CAST POTTERY AND CERAMICS

Moulded and slip cast pottery and ceramics

David Cowley

B T BATSFORD LTD   LONDON

ACKNOWLEDGMENT

I wish to thank the following who have helped in the preparation of this book: the students of Whitelands College, Audrey Walker and the students of the Barry Summer School course 'Fibres and Clay' 1974–1976, and all those who have contributed examples of their work.

For the care and trouble they took with the photographs I am especially grateful to: Tony Youles for figures 48, 50, 51, 58, 81, 82, 83, 84, 101, 102, 103, 113, 114, 121, 122, 123, Lawrence Gresswell for figures 46, 52, 53, 54, 55, 56, 98, 99, 100, 104, 110, 111, 112, 116, 125, Barbara McPherson for figures 36, 37, 45, 47, 49, and Derek Scarbrough for the cover photograph.

Finally I would like to thank my wife Jyl, Phyllis Fountain, and Thelma M. Nye of Batsford who have patiently given much invaluable help and encouragement.

First published 1978
First published in paperback 1984
ISBN 0 7134 0971 1 (hardback)
ISBN 0 7134 0972 X (paperback)

Filmset by
Servis Filmsetting Ltd, Manchester
Printed in Great Britain by
The Anchor Press Ltd, Tiptree, Essex
for the publishers
B T Batsford Ltd
4 Fitzhardinge Street
London W1H 0AH

CONTENTS

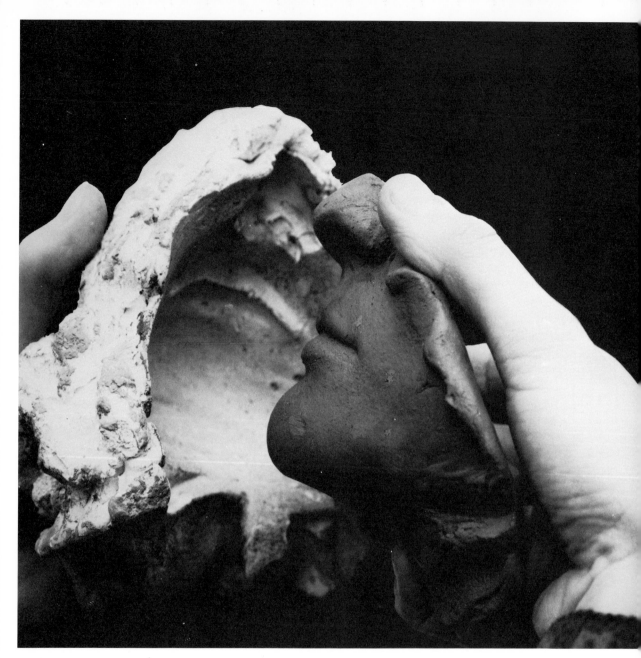

1

INTRODUCTION

Clay can be formed into objects by processes that are either *direct*, which include modelling, throwing and various types of handbuilding, or processes that are *indirect*, which involve moulding. As the application of pressure to limit the movement of plastic clay is an essential part of any ceramic forming process, some aspect of moulding in its widest sense must occur at some time. Whether it is done by the naked hand, a wooden or metal tool or a mould, is of minor importance. However, there seems to exist in the minds of many people a positive division or separation and indeed a qualitative implication, between direct and indirect forming processes. 'Direct processes are essentially creative, while indirect ones are sterile and only fit for industrial mass production.' 'Moulding is a recognized industrial technique, but it has little value to the craftsman or artist.' Statements like this are often found in books dealing with ceramics. This attitude is perpetuated by those who are content merely to fill and re-fill commercially produced moulds without any creative attempt to use or modify the cast forms produced from them. They seem totally oblivious of the creativity that can be involved in mould making, or indeed that the making of a mould can be an integral part of the total creative process.

Multiple-piece moulds that need highly skilled knowledge, complicated machinery and sophisticated equipment are not within the scope of this book, neither is the making of moulds for mass production. It does not deal with the technicalities of ceramic firing and decorating techniques which can be found in many excellent books. Instead the emphasis will be on the creative opportunities afforded to children, students, and others starting to work in clay, by the use of simple one and two piece moulds. In other words an introduction to the imaginative, inventive and creative use of moulds for individual expression rather than moulds for the production of multiple, repeatable complex commercial forms.

It must be emphasised that the description of processes, their development, their uses and related ideas and suggestions are not the only ones possible and should not be slavishly and blindly followed. They are only indications of how press moulding and slip casting can be used. Obviously, there are certain basic principles and fundamentals, that are crucial, but all techniques and processes need to be modified for personal requirements and creative and expressive development.

Press Moulded Ceramics

The earliest ceramic containers or pottery forms are generally associated with a simple moulding technique – that of smearing the inside of a basket with a layer of plastic clay. Fire would then be used to burn away the basket or 'mould', leaving a hardened clay shell. Whether or not this was the true beginning of pottery, it serves to illustrate the fundamental technique of moulding. That is, that clay pressed into or over a shape will take on the form that it comes into contact with and will retain it, even when the 'mould' and the clay are separated. A concave form determines the outer surface of the moulded shape, whilst a convex form determines the inner shape. In either case the plastic clay pressed into or over the form is allowed to stiffen slightly before separating it from the moulding agent.

Simple, one piece moulds were used all over the ancient Middle East, Greece, Rome and China, while two piece moulds are thought to be classical in origin. Especially beautiful pieces of moulding are found in fifth century BC Greece, third century BC Tanagra grave figures, and Pre-Tang China, Ming Chi funeral figures. While at the other extreme, complex and elaborate multiple piece moulds are associated with the work of Meissen and other European factories in the eighteenth century.

The vast majority of mass produced ceramics today, that is, domestic tableware, sanitary ware, technical and electrical components, are moulded or cast. In fact, industrial mass production by its very nature needs to employ highly complicated, sophisticated and refined moulding and casting techniques.

2   Press mould and cast. Vera Cruz, Mexico

BASIC PRINCIPLES

Press moulding involves pressing plastic clay against the 'face' or sides of the mould to achieve a form or cast. Plastic clay is clay that is soft and pliable enough to fill easily all the hollows, indentations and cavities of a mould and yet is stiff enough to retain its shape when it is removed from the mould. If the clay is too soft and sticky, it is difficult to obtain a sharp and clear impression from the mould, or to remove it reasonably quickly without it losing its shape. However, if the clay is too hard and stiff, it is difficult to fill the mould without exerting excessive pressure, or prevent the clay cracking as it is pressed into the mould.

So if plastic clay is pressed into a hollow or pressed over a hump, the clay will take on and retain that shape when separated from the hollow or hump, after allowing it to stiffen slightly. See figures 3a and b.

It is essential for moulds not to have any areas of *undercutting* otherwise the cast cannot be separated from the mould without it being distorted. It is essential to understand the principle of undercutting as this is crucial to the efficient making of moulds. Forms within a mould that prevent the easy withdrawal or separation of the cast from the mould are known as *undercuts*. Either these must be eliminated or be taken into consideration when the mould or moulds are being made. Figures 4a and b may help to clarify undercutting.

One piece moulds produce what is essentially a relief, because it has only one 'face' that is created by the mould. although a 'back' may be added later to complete the total form.

Two piece moulds produce a complete three dimensional form without any finishing or additions. The second piece consists of a 'back' to complete the 'front' made by the first piece. Two piece press moulds are usually filled with clay independently and joined together to make up the complete form.

In some cases a totally three dimensional form can be achieved by joining two casts from the same press mould.

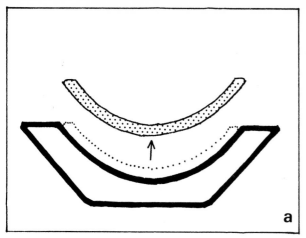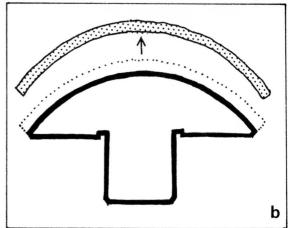

3　*a*　Cross section of hollow press mould and cast　　　*b*　Cross section of hump press mould and cast

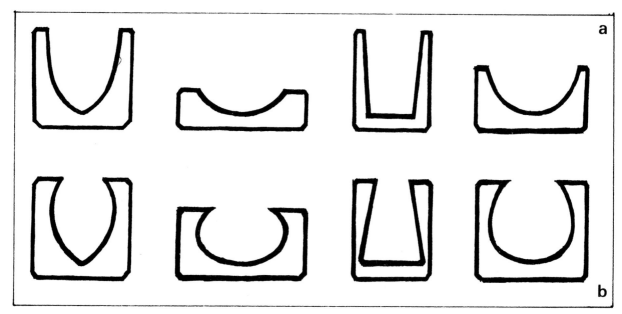

4　*a*　Cross sections of hollow press moulds without undercutting
　　b　Cross sections of hollow press moulds containing undercutting

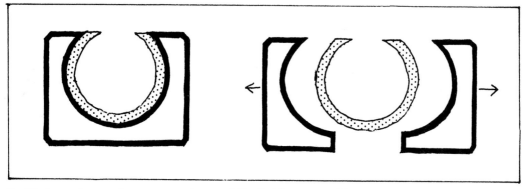

5　Undercutting can be overcome by carefully dividing a mould

Ceramic moulds need to be made of a porous material so the mould will absorb moisture from the clay cast. This drying and subsequent shrinkage makes the easy withdrawal of the clay from the cast possible, and its handling without the loss of its shape, soon after casting. The most common press moulds are those made from clay hardened in a bisque firing, or from plaster of paris. The latter are the most extensively used because they are easily and cheaply made, relatively light so easily transportable and are highly absorbent. The disadvantages are that they are fragile and are easily chipped or broken and have a more limited life than bisque moulds.

The mould is made from the *master* or *model*, which is the final intended form of the cast. The model is usually solid and must be made larger than the required finished cast, because of the shrinkage of the cast during drying and firing. See figure 6.

The *model* is usually made of clay or plaster, but other materials and 'found' objects like storage containers, packages, pieces of machinery, and electric light bulbs, can also be used. Models made from plaster of paris can be produced on a lathe, a turning box, or powered wheel, if symmetrical forms are wanted, or they can be freely modelled or carved. For the beginner it is often best to start by making a simple model with plastic clay. The clay can be freely modelled, formed on a pottery wheel, or shaped in any way, providing there is no undercutting. It is often better if the clay is allowed to harden slightly before putting the finishing touches to the surface prior to making the mould from it.

The simplest and most commonly used one piece moulds are those used to produce dish-like forms, known as hollow press moulds if they are concave in form, or hump moulds if they are convex in form. In a hollow press mould the outside surface of the dish is determined by the mould, in a hump mould it is the inside surface.

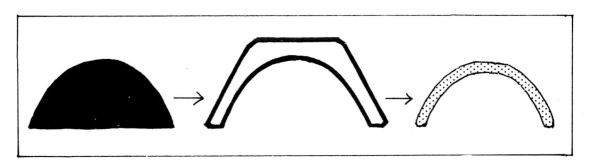

6   Cross sections of model, mould, and cast

7 Hump and hollow press moulds

Making a hollow plaster press mould

1   Preferably using a clay that does not contain grog or sand, the model is shaped in solid form on to a piece of hardboard or a similarly smooth surfaced and flexible material. This sheet of hardboard should be at least 76–102 mm (3–4 in.) bigger than the clay model resting on it. Before making the model it is often useful to draw carefully its circumference onto the surface of the hardboard. Avoid sharp corners and any undercuts on the model and where its edges touch the hardboard. Make certain there is a crisp edge and again no undercuts. See figure 8.

2   The model, shaped in plastic clay, is left to harden slightly before scraping and finishing it to achieve the required form and surface. A template can be useful in achieving an even and all over profile. See figure 9. The important thing is not to be impatient but spend some time carefully and methodically working on the form until you arrive at exactly what you need.

3   Build up a wall of thick clay about 38–64 mm ($1\frac{1}{2}$–2 in.) from the edges of the model that touch the hardboard and at least 50 mm (2 in.) higher than the tallest part of the model. This wall, which is sometimes known as a *cottle*, can also be made of lino or cardboard. A wooden casting box can also be used to contain the liquid plaster of paris that is to be poured over the model. See figures 10a and b. Whatever is used, it is essential to seal any gaps from the inside with plastic clay.

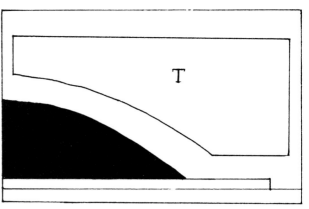

8 Cross section of unsatisfactory profile of a model, showing undercutting and excessively sharp edges

9 Cross section of satisfactory profile with template (T)

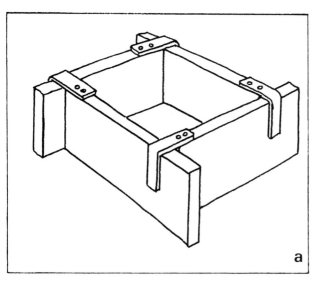

a

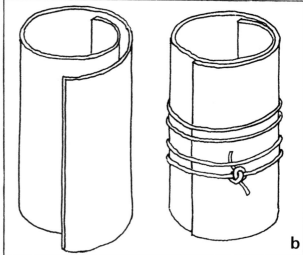

b

10 Types of cottles.
a Wooden casting box. The surfaces should be oiled regularly to prevent plaster sticking to them
b A sheet of linoleum, or thick cardboard. The string can be tightened with a pencil or a block of wood can be wedged between the cottle and the string

11 Cross section of finished model with attached cottle (C) and clay seams (CS)
The liquid plaster can either be filled to level (A), or when the cottle is half full, plaster can be scooped from the edges to cover the exposed areas of the model, covering it with an even layer (B)

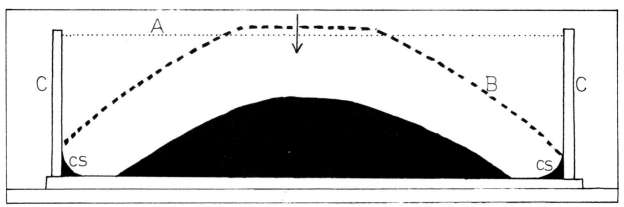

4 *Mix the plaster of paris* Half fill a plastic bowl or bucket with water (make certain that there will be enough of the completed plaster mix to cover the model with at least a 38–64 mm ($1\frac{1}{2}$–2 in.) layer. Adding additional plaster mix when you discover that you do not have sufficient to cover the model is never very satisfactory in the making of plaster moulds). Sprinkle the plaster onto the water lightly but fairly quickly until an 'island' is formed. Continue shaking the plaster around the edges until it is lying just below the surface of the water. Some people prefer to weigh or measure the plaster and water – before mixing them, usually in the proportion of 3 plaster : 2 water or or 1·7 kg plaster to 710 ml water (3 lb 12 oz plaster to 2 pints water). To avoid creating any bubbles while mixing, slide a hand to the bottom of the container and quickly stir from the bottom, until a lump free mixture is obtained.

5 Immediately pour into the cottle, though some people prefer to wait for the plaster to thicken slightly, and cover the model with an even 38–64 mm ($1\frac{1}{2}$–2 in.) layer or fill the cottle until the plaster is 38–64 mm ($1\frac{1}{2}$–2 in.) above the highest part of the model. See figure 11. (The thickness of this plaster layer should naturally vary with the size of the model, but for most moulds up to 25–30 cm (10–12 in.) in diameter, this thickness is satisfactory.) When filled, slap or agitate the plaster mould to force it into all hollows and remove any trapped air bubbles or pockets. As the plaster starts to set level the top surface to create a flat base for the plaster mould when it is inverted.

6 Leave the plaster of paris to set for about 20–30 minutes, but not for a long period as it becomes difficult to separate dry clay from most plaster moulds. Remove the cottle and clay seams and carefully separate the plaster mould from the clay model. Surform or file all sharp edges on the outside of the mould that might chip when it is dry and in use. See figure 12. Leave the mould to dry slowly and evenly. Do not force dry moulds over kilns or heaters as this often makes them weak and unsatisfactory. Remember always to return all clay used in the making of moulds to a separate container from those that are used for making kiln fired objects. Even the smallest piece of plaster of paris can badly damage a ceramic object. Other points to remember when using plaster of paris are: Mix the plaster in clean flexible plastic containers which are the easiest to clean. Always add plaster to water, never water to powder. Avoid adding more water or plaster once the mixture has been stirred as this weakens the final cast. The water used should be at room temperature. If it is too cold the plaster takes much longer to set, whilst if it is too hot the plaster will set before there is time to pour it over the model. Lastly, any plaster washed down a sink will clog the pipes. Everything that has to be cleaned should be washed in a bucket filled with water. Once the plaster has settled at the bottom of the bucket, decant the water and throw away the solid plaster pieces.

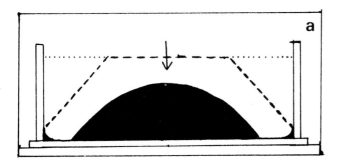

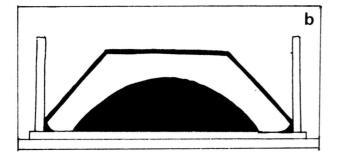

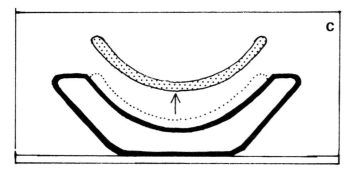

12 Cross sections of the stages in the making of a hollow press mould
a Model with cottle around it before the plaster is poured
b Model covered with a layer of plaster
c Inverted, surformed, and dried mould with cast from it

Making a hump plaster press mould

1   The use of a hollow press mould described above is probably the easiest and most efficient way of producing the model for a hump mould, though the required hollow form can be easily carved out of a solid block of plastic clay. If clay is used, make certain that the outside thickness or 'wall' is thick enough (about 50–75 mm (2–3 in.)) to hold the liquid plaster of paris that will be poured into the hollow. See figure 13a. If the hollow form is made of a material other than plastic clay, it should be coated with a *separator* (soft soap, oil, vaseline, or very thin slip) to prevent that material sticking to the plaster of paris.

2   Make a cylinder out of cardboard (this will vary with the size of the mould, but roughly 127 mm (5 in.) long and about 102 mm (4 in.) in diameter for a mould 25–30 cm (10–12 in.) in diameter) which will eventually form the stand for the mould. See figure 13b.

3   Mix the plaster of paris as described earlier and pour into the hollow form of the model. Sink the cardboard cylinder to about 12 mm ($\frac{1}{2}$ in.) into the top surface of the plaster when it is slightly stiffer, and fill it with plaster of paris. The cylinder which creates a stand for the hump mould, is not absolutely necessary, though it certainly makes a hump mould easier to use. Instead of this stand, the mould could rest on a brick or a large tin filled with sand to weight it.

4   Let the plaster of paris set thoroughly, remove the cardboard and remove the clay or separate the hollow press mould from the hump mould, if this was used. Surform or file the outer edges of the hump mould and leave it to dry slowly. See figure 13c.

As hump moulds shape the inside form and surface of the cast, designs can be carved into the plaster. These carved designs are transferred to the cast form as low relief decoration.

13   Cross sections of the stages in the making of a hump mould
a   Hollow form carved into a block of clay. Plaster is then poured to level (A)
b   Cardboard tube (CT) in position and plaster poured to level (B)
c   Inverted, surformed, and dried mould and cast from it

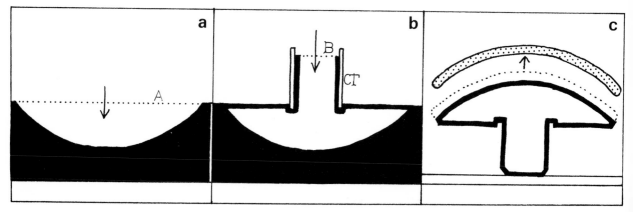

14   Mould made from pouring liquid plaster into the hollow formed by two hands

Other materials besides clay or plaster can be used to form the model. Fine damp sand, contained in a low wooden box, can be compressed into a dome or hump to form a hollow press mould in plaster, or a hollow in the sand will produce a hump mould. Liquid plaster of paris poured into or over fruit, vegetable and egg containers, or packing separators, will produce moulds of both types. Try pouring liquid plaster of paris into or over part of your body, previously coated with vaseline to prevent the plaster sticking to the skin. Crumpled fabrics, paper, and cardboard, bags of plastic filled with sand or sawdust and stones and gourds can act as models. There are numerous and fascinating ways of achieving different types and variations of basic hollow and hump press moulds of plaster of paris.

15   Objects that could be used as models for moulds

ONE PIECE BISQUE PRESS MOULDS

Bisque moulds are more hardwearing and durable than those made from plaster of paris, but they are heavier and less absorbent, so they have a slower output. They are mainly used for the production of elaborate applied ornament, or applique pieces in the form of sprigging, low reliefs and simple figures where plaster moulds would not retain fine detail over continued use.

The clay to be used for the mould can be worked in any of the traditional ceramic forming processes. It can be thrown on a wheel, coiled or handbuilt, carved, modelled or pressed over a 'found' object. However, the method that will be described is probably the most suitable for the beginner. Whatever method, or clay is used, it is vital to allow for shrinkage in the firing of the mould as well as the cast from it.

Clay containing grog is the most suitable for the making of bisque moulds as this allows for a mould that is thicker and more durable, as well as having walls of uneven thicknesses. Consequently, the concave inside form can be different to the convex or outside form. In fact, both surfaces can be used for press moulding. A hump and a hollow press mould in one form. However, if the clay is too heavily grogged obviously fine detail cannot be achieved from the mould.

18

1   From a solid block of clay, shape the outside or convex surface of the mould, making certain that air is not trapped in the clay while it is worked. Allow the shape to dry slightly and stiffen before scraping and finishing the surface. Flatten part of the top surface, this will act as a base when the form is inverted.

2   When it is almost leather hard and stiff enough to retain its shape, invert the form, resting it on the previously made base, or if the form is curved, a pad of sponge foam rubber or soft material. Scoop out the inside or concave form required. Remember that moulds made of fine clays should not have a thickness greater than about 12 mm ($\frac{1}{4}$ in.), while heavily grogged clays can have thickness of up to 64–76 mm ($2\frac{1}{2}$–3 in.). See figures 16a, b, c and d.

3   Allow the mould to dry slowly and thoroughly and bisque fire in the usual way to a temperature of about 1100°C.

'Found' objects can also be used to create bisque moulds. Carefully pressing objects like stones, shells, childrens' toys, pieces of machinery, hands, elbows and knees into blocks of plastic clay will produce negatives of those forms. When dried and bisque fired, these negatives will reproduce positives, or replicas of the original, if plastic clay is pressed into them.

Certain objects, particularly those made of metal, tend to stick to clay, leaving a poor impression or cast. In such cases use a slightly stiffer clay and brush the metal object repeatedly with talc or fine sand. After the object has been carefully withdrawn, leave the clay to stiffen before trimming off any excess clay and evening out the walls.

16   Cross sections in the making of a one piece bisque mould
a   Exterior form is modelled in clay
b   When inverted the interior is carved from the solid block
    Rest the mould on a piece of foam rubber (F) to avoid distortion
c   Hollow press mould when the interior is used for casting
d   Hump mould when inverted and the exterior is used

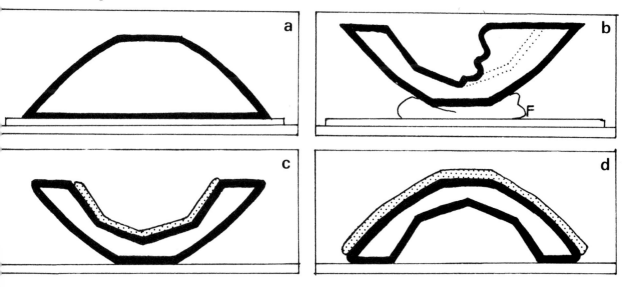

Naturally it is best to keep the number of pieces that make up a complete mould to a minimum, but it is useless to try and cut down the number of pieces if a model warrants it; the need for a two piece mould is explained in figures 17a–f, dealing with a mould for a sphere.

The dividing line drawn on the model, or master, is known as the *dividing line* or *parting seam* of the mould. This is the line from which the mould sections can be separated or withdrawn in opposite directions.

A mould consisting of two pieces can also be used to achieve a required thickness of form, instead of the pieces acting as the formers of the outer surface. See figure 19.

17   a   Sphere is completely encased by plaster block
       b   Plaster block is divided along the diameter of the sphere or parting seam
       c   Two pieces are separated freeing the sphere
The position of the seam is crucial. It must be along the widest part of the form
       d   Incorrect position of seam, model is caught in plaster block
       e   Correct position of seam
       f   Incorrect position of seam

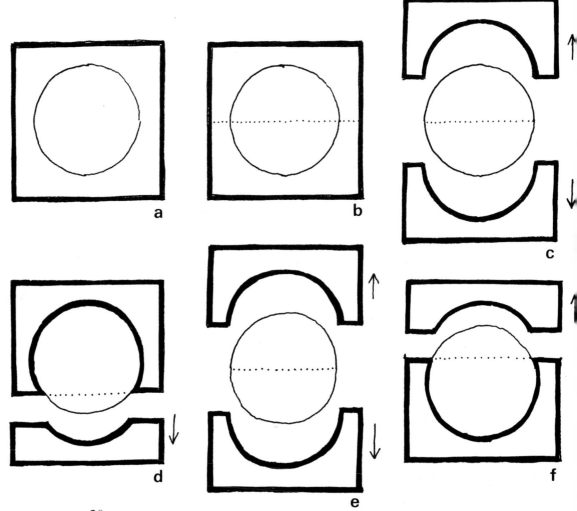

a

b

c

d

e

f

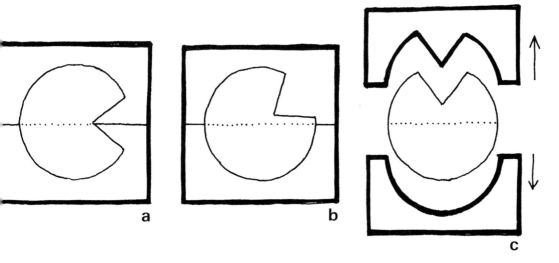

18 The seam must divide the model in two but its position must be carefully considered in relation to the particular form
a and *b* Incorrect position
c Correct position

19 A mould consisting of two pieces can also be used to achieve a required thickness of form, instead of the pieces acting purely as formers for the exterior surface

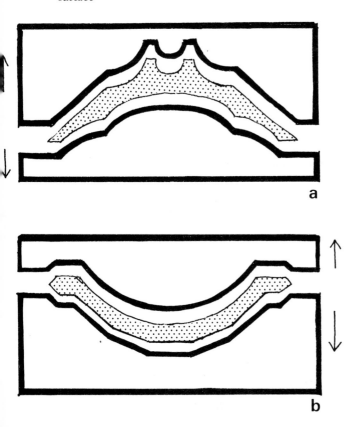

Making a two piece plaster mould

1 *Find the dividing line or parting seam on the model*

Method A Look carefully at the model and try visualizing where the parting seam for the two separate pieces could be located avoiding any undercutting. It is essential to move the model around and see it from all angles while doing this. Make a rough visual approximation with a pencil or mark the line in some way.

To find the actual parting line on the model, place it on a level surface, with the approximation of the parting seam horizontal and parallel to that surface. Rest the model on a small pad or lump of clay which will hold the model in position, yet allow it to be shifted and altered if need be. Check there is no undercutting by looking onto the model from directly above, making certain you can see all the surface from that position. If you cannot, move the model until this is possible. When the model is in the right position, rub one entire edge of a square with a soft or indelible pencil, and holding the model firmly, move the edge around it. Make certain that the edge is in an upright position and that the other edge is always on the level surface. The edge that touches the model will leave a pencil mark on the high spots of it. This trace is the parting line for the two moulds. See figure 20.

20

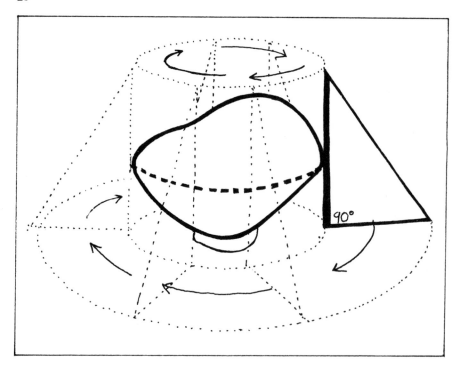

Method B Fix the model firmly, making certain it is resting vertically, in the middle of a series of circles one inch apart and dissected by two lines at 90° to one another. See figure 21a.

With a pair of compasses draw a series of arcs on the surface of the model using lines A. See figure 21b. Join the points where the arcs intersect with an indelible pencil. Do the same on the opposite side of the model using lines B. Join the two lines on the top surface.

The continuous line on the surface of the model is the parting seam for the two moulds. This second method is most suitable for symmetrical forms turned on a lathe or wheel. Both methods should only be used after you are certain that a two piece mould is required.

These are complicated processes for the beginner and it is often preferable to begin by using a one piece mould twice and joining these symmetrical casts together or by making your two piece mould from a mass produced 'found' object. Especially useful are plastic forms that have been cast or moulded and whose parting seams are still visible. These seams indicate where the plaster moulds should be divided.

Finding the parting seams for multiple piece moulds needs much experience and is outside the scope of this book. However, if these interest you, start with simple one and two piece moulds and gradually work up to more complicated ones. Remember that only the general principles of undercutting and angles of withdrawal can be relied on to guide you. Not all parting seams appear on the most prominent forms of the model and above all, keep the number of pieces to a minimum.

21 *a* Plan of diagram on which model will rest
  b A pair of compasses being used to draw a series of arcs on a model

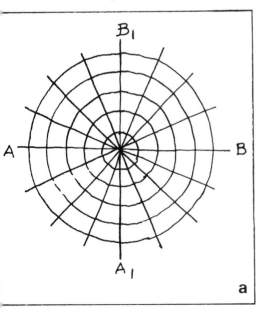

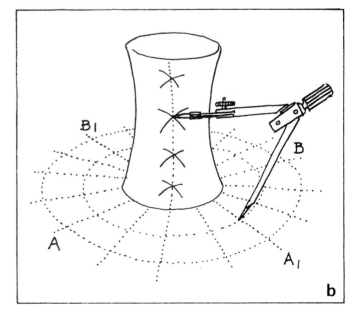

2   Having established the parting seam, place the model on a small pad or cushion of clay with the parting seam horizontal and parallel to the working surface and the base, if there is one, vertical. The whole thing should be on a rigid wooden board at least 76–102 mm (3–4 in.) larger than the model. Build up plastic clay around the model until it is level with the parting seam. Carefully smooth this clay bed surrounding the model, making certain that the clay extends horizontally from it to the edge of the board. Models of plastic clay do not need a separator but most other surfaces do, in which case, coat the model with a thin application of separator (soft soap, vaseline, oil, slip or any other suitable medium) but avoid too thick a coat as this will mark the surface of the model.

3   Place walls of clay, cardboard, wood or lino around the clay. These walls or cottle should be at least 50 mm (2 in.) above the highest part of the model and at least 38–64 mm (1½–2 in.) from the edge of the model. Mark a line 38–64 mm (1½–2 in.) from the highest part of the model on the inside of the cottle, the line up to which the liquid plaster will be poured. Clamp the walls if they are of wood, firmly tie if they are of cardboard or lino, and make certain all joints are seamed from the inside, to prevent the plaster escaping. See figure 22. Mix the plaster of paris and pour carefully over the model and inside the cottle until it reaches the level previously marked. Avoid trapping air as you pour and gently shake the table, tap the sides of the cottle or slap the surface of the plaster to bring any air bubbles to the surface. Let the plaster set for about 20–30 minutes.

4   Remove the walls carefully and invert the whole thing so that the plaster is now resting on the work surface. Remove the wooden board and the clay bed, being very careful *not to separate the model from the plaster*.

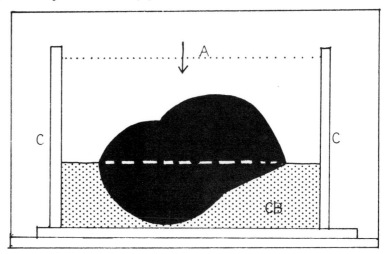

22   Model is placed in clay bed (CB) up to the parting seam, and surrounded by cottle (C) Plaster is poured to level (A)

5   Cut low depressions known as *keys* in the plaster surface, either on the edge or nearer the model. See figures 23*a* and *b*.

These *keys are to locate mould sections together and prevent any movement between the two faces of the moulds.* The depressions cut in the first section with a teaspoon or coin or round sectioned surform or file, are filled with plaster when making the second section of the mould forming humps in that mould. When the plaster has set and then separated the humps on one section will correspond to the hollows or depressions on the other. When ready for casting, mould sections can be easily aligned by the fitting together of hump with depression. See figures 23*c* and *d*, 24*a* to *c*.

(Sometimes a 'spare' can also be made by cutting a groove in the plaster around the seam, and filling this with a roll or coil of clay before pouring over the second layer of plaster. See figures 25*a* and *b*. 'Spares' are not always necessary with press moulds, but are essential with slip cast moulds and will be discussed in a later section.)

23   Type of keys
a   Cut on the edges of the first piece of the mould with a round file or surform
b   Cut into the top surface of the first piece of the mould with a coin or spoon
c   Cross section of efficient key forms
d   Cross section of unsatisfactory key forms, showing poor angle of withdrawal, and excessive depth so they are liable to break

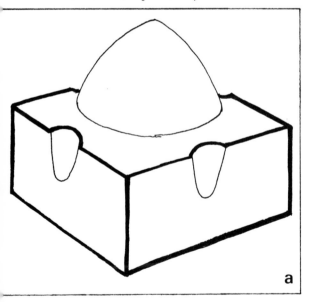

a

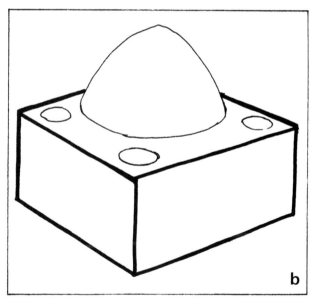

b

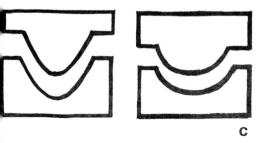

c

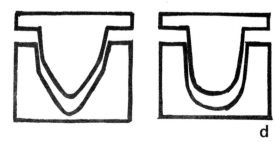

d

24 *a* Keys on the edge of a mould are usually made with a curved or round sectioned file or surform
b Keys in the top surface of the first piece of the mould are usually cut with a small spoon or coin held vertically and twisted into the plaster. Avoid cutting too deeply and creating undercutting
c It is useful to vary the size and avoid a regular arrangement of keys for quicker visual alignment

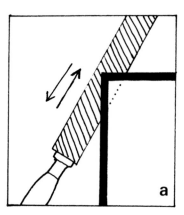

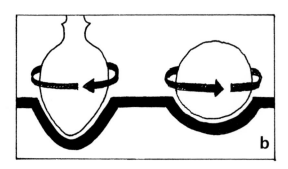

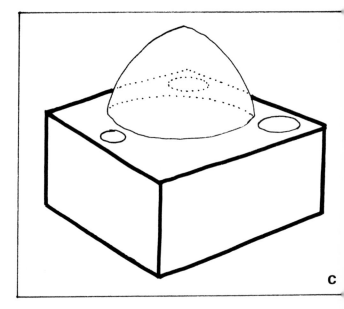

25 *a* The spare is made by cutting a semi-circular channel around the seam into the first piece of the mould and filling it with a coil of clay (C) before pouring the plaster for the second piece
b Cross section of two piece mould showing coil (C)

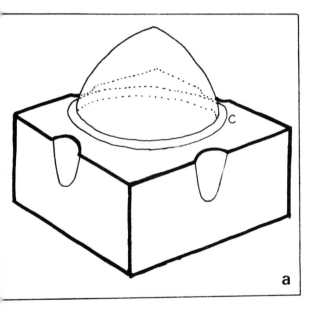

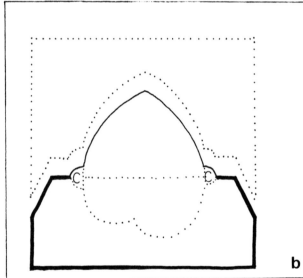

6 *Apply a separator to all surfaces of the plaster and to the model if this is necessary*. Build another wall as before, seam all the joints, pour in the plaster as before and leave it to set. See figure 26.

26 Cross section of inverted model and first piece of mould with keys cut into top surface. Plaster is poured to level (A)

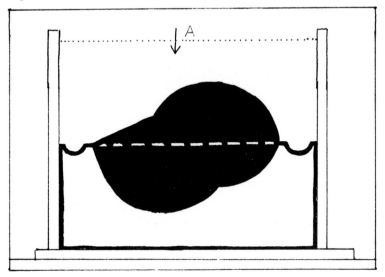

7 Remove the walls and seams and very carefully separate the two halves of the mould. If this is difficult, leave a tap to drip onto the line where the two moulds join, or if this still does not work, leave the mould to dry overnight and then try again. When separated, carefully remove the model and wash away all the traces of the separator with a very soft brush.

8 Relocate the two pieces of the mould and fix them firmly together with thick rubber bands, or strips of rubber cut from the section of the inner tube of a car tyre. Trim the outside edges to an angle of about 45° and round them off if you wish, with a surform or file. It is very important to do this as it prevents the plaster chipping and spoiling the clay being used to take a cast. Allow the moulds to dry slowly. Do not force dry them on a kiln or radiator.

Whenever possible the mould should be of an even thickness, to facilitate equal and even absorbtion. A thicker plaster section will absorb more moisture from a clay cast than a thin plaster section which is soon saturated.

27 Cross section of separated model, mould and cottle

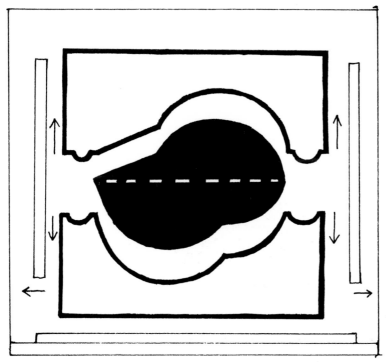

Making a two piece bisque mould

The procedure is much the same as that used to make a two piece plaster mould, except that plastic clay is used instead of plaster of paris and the mould is finally hardened by a bisque firing. Two piece bisque moulds are not usually as efficient at reproducing such fine detail as their plaster equivalents, but are certainly very useful for multiple reproduction of basic shapes, that can be worked upon. Details and refinements being added in terms of applied surfaces or carvings into the surface of the cast. The great advantage of bisque moulds lies in their strength and durability.

1 Gradually press the model into a lump of clay up to its parting line or seam. Remove at intervals while doing this to check the quality of the impression being made in the clay. If the mould is of a non-absorbent material, especially metal, dust with talc or fine sand between each pressing and removal. This prevents it and the plastic clay sticking together. Trim off the excess clay leaving 25–38 mm (1–1½ in.) thickness around the model but remember the thickness is obviously dependent upon the type of clay being used. See figure 28a.

2 Level off the top surface of the clay bed making certain it is level with the parting line. Carve or trim the outside edge of the clay into a series of curved surfaces, but make certain that the clay near the model is untouched. See figure 28b. These curves act as keys for the locating of the two pieces of the mould and are usually more satisfactory in this instance than the small keys made with coins in plaster piece moulds.

3 Dust the model and the top surface of the clay with talc or fine sand (the equivalent of a separator) and leave to stiffen and dry slightly, before covering with another lump of plastic clay, which will act as the second piece of the mould. Press this clay against the model and the other clay mould being careful not to distort it or trap air between them. Trim off the excess clay as before and flatten the top surface to act as a base when the second piece of the mould is inverted. See figure 28c.

4 Leave to dry and stiffen slightly, separate the two pieces of the mould from each other and the model and put aside to dry thoroughly before bisque firing. While in its plastic state handle the clay with great care and only when absolutely necessary, otherwise distortions will occur in the mould.

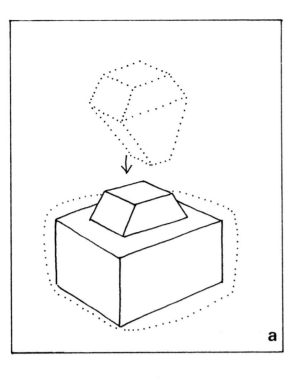

a

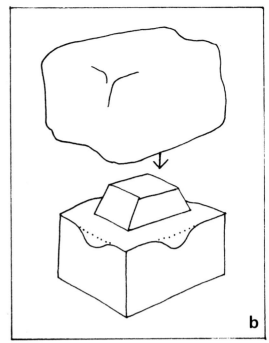

b

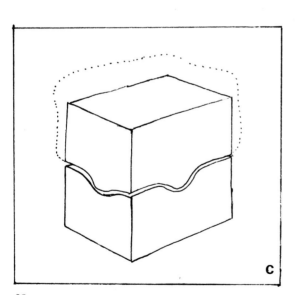

c

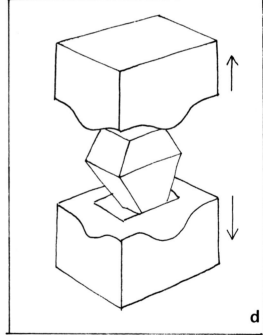

d

28

29 Barry Summer School

MOULDS FROM OTHER MATERIALS

Besides the traditional one and two piece press moulds made of plaster of paris or bisque fired clay there is a wealth of 'moulds' or 'formers' for plastic clay that can be found around us. These 'found' objects are particularly useful because they can have the advantage of expanding our vision and concept of moulds and moulded forms. There is a danger that we make moulds that are merely repeats of well-known and proven mould forms. However, forms not usually associated with mould making may help us to re-examine our concepts and ideas of moulds. Sometimes these 'forming agents' are more flexible and can be more easily altered in shape or modified than a plaster of paris or bisque mould. For example, a paper, plastic or fabric bag filled with sawdust, sand, or polystyrene granules, when it is being used as a 'mould', can easily be altered in shape to provide a great variety of moulded forms. Besides, such bags, large stones, shells, gourds, fruit and vegetables, pieces of machinery and electrical components, hands, elbows, knees and other parts of the body, crumpled paper card or fabrics, and inflated balloons are just some of the 'found' objects that can provide fascinating 'moulds' for slabs of plastic clay.

30 Barry Summery School

PREPARATION OF CLAY FOR PRESS MOULDING

The forming process does determine and demand certain properties of the clay being used. Clay that is formed on a wheel usually needs to be very plastic, while excessive plasticity is usually a disadvantage when moulding or casting. Plastic clays have a high shrinkage and tend to warp considerably if not dried evenly and carefully. It is unlikely that a clay that is suitable for casting will also be satisfactory for throwing on a wheel.

Some clays are so plastic and pliable that they can be 'stretched' and bent with little cracking or breaking, while others are so 'short' and crumbly that they can easily be compressed into a mass but are almost impossible to 'stretch' and bend satisfactorily. *It is the particle size more than any other factor which determines the plasticity of a clay. A generalisation is that the smaller the particle, the greater the plasticity.*

Most clays, except those that are highly plastic, are suitable for press moulding, although those that contain some *grog* (small particles of fired clay) or sand, are usually the most favoured. The larger the mould the more heavily grogged the clay should be, to avoid uneven drying and warpage. However, the clay being used depends on the nature and quality of the mould. Naturally a heavily grogged clay would be unsuitable for a finely detailed mould.

The clay to be press moulded should be wedged or kneaded in the usual way to remove any impurities and any air pockets until it is soft and pliable enough to enter the hollows and cavities of the mould without excessive pressure, yet be stiff and firm enough to retain its shape soon after pressing. Experience will soon determine when the clay is in the 'right' condition. However, for the beginner a simple test is to take a handful of clay and roll it between the palms of your hands until you have a roll or coil about 25 mm (1 in.) in diameter and about 102 mm (4 in.) long. If you can bend the clay until the ends touch without too many cracks appearing, it should be plastic enough. Too many cracks and the roll breaking means the clay is too dry and needs to be softened by the gradual addition of water while continuing to wedge or knead. Another simple test is to take a lump of clay and squeeze it between your fingers. If the clay comes away easily and cleanly from your fingers without sticking to them, then it is in a reasonable condition. If the clay sticks to your fingers, continue to wedge or knead it on a plaster or similarly absorbent surface until it is stiffer.

It is not always necessary for clay to be in a plastic condition when press moulding. An idea may find its best expression in forms that have a cracked and broken quality when they are removed from the mould. In such cases leather hard, heavily grogged, or clays of varying consistencies can be used. However, cracks in a moulded surface tend to weaken the object, so you need to experiment and find the most suitable solution for the idea being expressed. But for most purposes clay in a soft, malleable condition is used to take a cast from a press mould.

TAKING A CAST FROM A ONE PIECE PRESS MOULD

1   The most efficient and widely used method of taking a cast from a press mould is to fill it with an even layer of clay that has been flattened or rolled to the required thickness, or cut from a block of clay.

Method A   Make certain you use enough clay to fill or cover the mould with the required thickness of clay. In most cases this is a layer of about 12–20 mm ($\frac{1}{2}$–$\frac{3}{4}$ in.) thick. It is not a good idea to add pieces of clay later if you discover there is insufficient clay for the mould you are using as there is always the risk of the form breaking where the clay has been added. It is always better to have too much clay rather than too little.

Thoroughly wedge or knead the clay and knock it into a compact mass, preferably a rough spherical shape, being careful not to trap any air in the clay while doing this. Place the clay on a piece of heavy canvas which should be larger than the slab you require. This canvas, or thick material prevents the clay sticking to the surface you are working on. Some people use drawing pins to fix the canvas to the working surface when flattening and rolling out the clay, but this is not necessary if the canvas is of a sufficiently heavy quality. Flatten the spherical form of clay by pressing down *evenly* on it from directly above with the palm of your hand (figure 31*a*). Invert the clay and continue to flatten gradually until the slab is about 50 mm (2 in.) thick. A stronger more compact slab of clay is produced if the clay is gradually flattened and inverted between each pressing. Vigorously beating a mass of clay with a rolling pin, only weakens the final clay slab and more often than not leads to air being trapped within the clay.

When the clay has been flattened evenly, a rolling pin can then be used to continue the process. Avoid directly using a rolling pin on a spherical form without first flattening it. This will only lead to difficulties. More control and pressure is possible if you roll from the middle of the slab to the edge furthest away from you, (figure 31*b*) turning the canvas through 180° between each rolling. Gradually roll out to the required thickness, continually inverting the clay and keeping in mind the shape needed to fill the mould. The final thickness can be judged visually or by wooden gauges of the right thickness. If gauges are being used, make certain that the ends of the rolling pin are directly over them when rolling out. See figure 31*c*.

Air pockets are trapped sometimes within the slab, either because of bad wedging or by inadvertently folding the clay on itself. If such air bubbles appear on the surface they should be pricked with a pottery needle and then smoothed over with a metal or rubber kidney. See figure 31*d*.

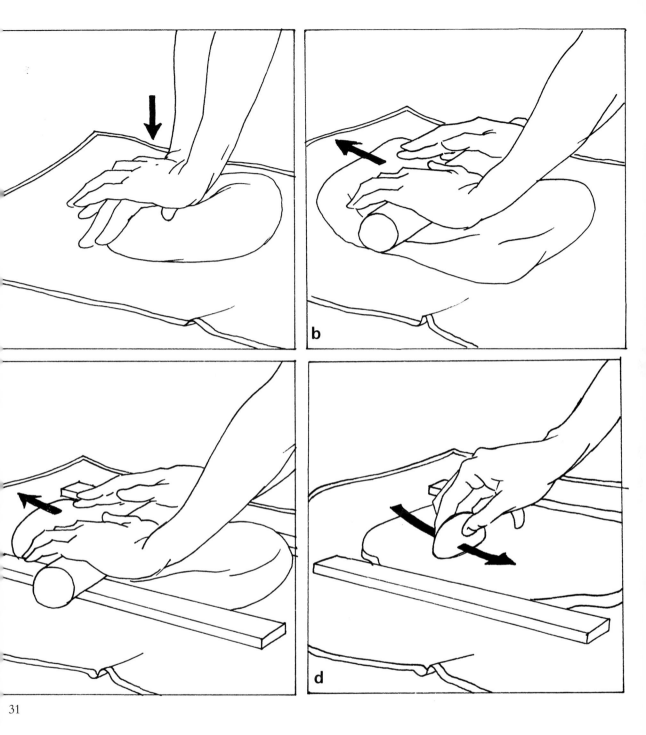

b

d

Method B   Prepare a large lump of clay and bang it on a bench until it is squared off and you have a rough cube. Place two gauges of the required thickness on either side of the clay and firmly resting a cutting wire on these gauges, drag it through the clay. It is important to hold the wire as taut as possible and the gauges firmly to the working surface. See figure 32*a*. Lift off the top block of clay and use the remaining slab to fill the mould. If more slabs are required repeat the process with the block. A cutting frame or *harp*, with an adjustable cutting wire can also be used to produce slabs of different thicknesses. See figures 32*b* and *c*.

Having produced the required slab of clay and pricked any air bubbles, smooth the top surface (the one which will go face downwards into the mould) with a metal or rubber kidney. A few drops of water on the clay will help in the smoothing.

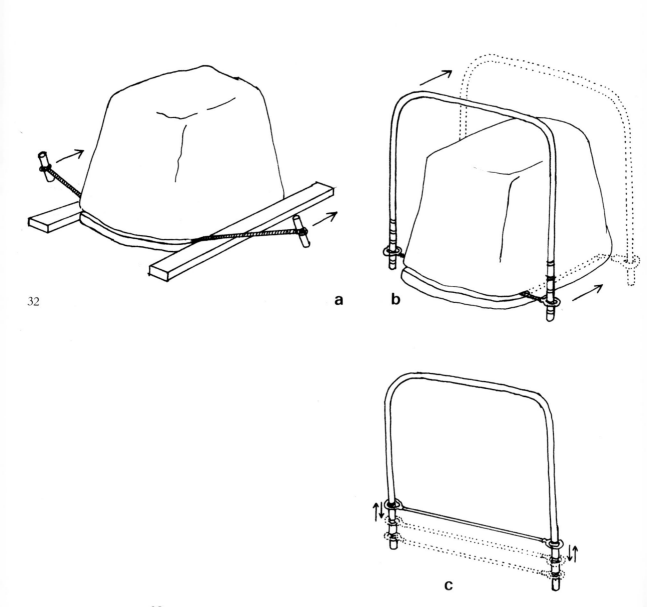

32

a   b

c

2   Lift the clay *and the canvas* together and gently lay the smoothed face downwards into the mould. Peel the canvas away from the clay and carefully start to work the slab into the sides of the mould pressing with a sponge or piece of foam rubber rather than your fingers as they tend to leave marks. Work slowly and methodically, being careful not to press the clay downwards into the mould without first lifting and loosening the slab from the edges of the mould. See figures 33*a* and *b*. If the slab is attached to the top edge of the mould when downward pressure is applied, it is stretched and consequently weakened. Always try to ease, rather than force clay slabs into a mould. Trim off any obviously unwanted clay and continue to ease the slab into the mould until it is flat against all surfaces of the mould.

33   *a*   Cross section of clay slab and canvas or fabric backing (F) being placed into the hollow press mould
b   Cross section showing how clay slab should be lifted at the edges (A) before pressing the clay into the mould (B)

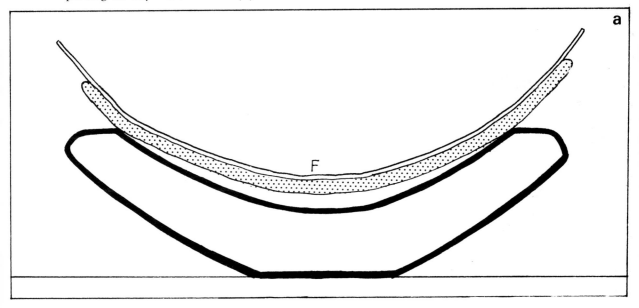

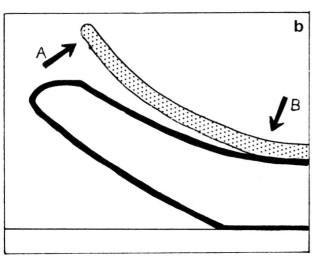

3 Trim excess clay level with the top edge of the mould, using a cutting wire or thin wooden modelling tool. Avoid metal tools as they can easily cause damage to plaster of paris moulds. Smooth exposed surfaces of the clay with a fine sponge or rubber kidney and check that the top edge of the clay case is not attached or stuck to the mould. If it is, the clay cannot sink into the mould as it dries and shrinks, without causing cracks and damage to the cast. A bevel cut with a modelling tool into the top edge of the cast, before it shrinks, is often useful to facilitate this. See figure 34.

The procedure for taking a cast from a hump press mould is much the same as above except the clay slab is eased over the mould rather than into it. See figure 35.

4 After the moulded form has been decorated or finished in the required manner, leave the cast to dry slowly and evenly, until it is stiff enough not to distort when it is removed from the mould. Do this by placing a rigid board over the mould before inverting it. Carefully lift off the mould leaving the cast resting on the board. Continue to dry it evenly and thoroughly after further finishing touches.

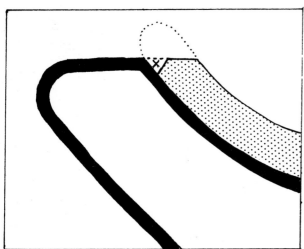

34 Cross section showing trimming of clay slab at the edges. Clay should be trimmed level with the top of the mould and a bevel (X) carefully cut at an angle of about 45°

35a Cross section of clay slab with canvas or fabric backing laid over hump mould
b Cross section of hump mould and clay slab, showing trimming of cast

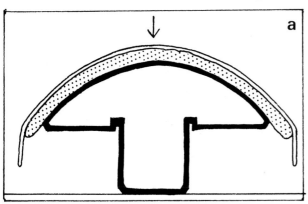
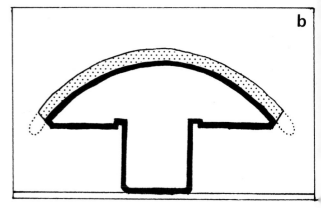

36 and 37   Eltham Green School

If the press mould is relatively small (102–127 mm (4–5 in.) in its longest dimension) and shallow (76–102 mm (3–4 in.) in depth) a solid lump of clay can also be used to fill the mould and the required thickness achieved by carving away the excess. When filling a small mould, be careful not to trap air between the mould and the clay being pressed into it. It is often best to press the clay firmly down in the centre of the mould gradually working outwards to the edges. See figure 38a. Once the mould is filled the excess can be removed with a wire loop. See figure 38b. For most clays a thickness of about 12 mm ($\frac{1}{2}$ in.), while those containing quantities of grog or sand may go to thickness of about 50–76 mm (2–3 in.).

When filling a deep or steep sided press mould use the method above or pinch a slightly smaller and thicker version of the final press moulded form. Place it in the mould and using a pad of material, foam rubber, or sponge attached to a stick, gently press the clay against the sides of the mould. Remove any excess clay with a wire loop. See figure 39. This method is far more satisfactory than trying to stretch a slab of clay into a deep mould.

If the press mould has a concave form which will produce a foot like shape on the press mould, the clay slab should be eased into the mould in the normal way, then an extra amount of clay should be carefully added to achieve a smooth inner profile or surface. When adding the extra clay make certain that it is firmly attached with slip and no air is trapped between the two layers of clay. See figure 40.

38   a   Cross section showing the filling of a small press mould with a sphere of clay
b   Cross section showing the trimming of the clay cast with a wire loop

a

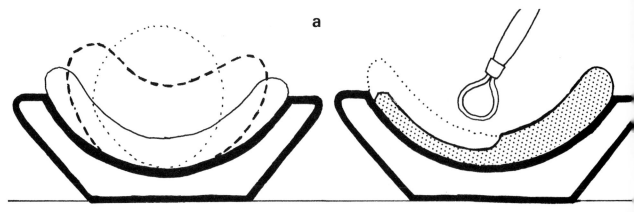

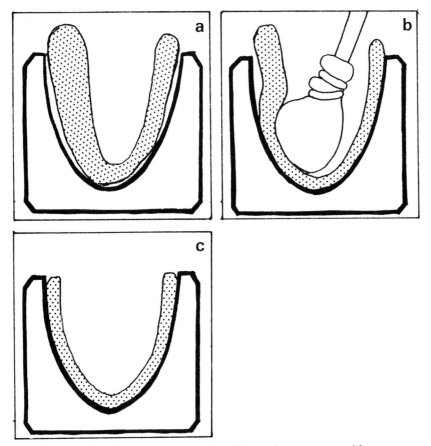

39   Cross sections showing the stages in filling a deep press mould
a   A pinched or thrown form is placed into the mould
b   The clay is carefully pressed against the sides of the mould using a foam rubber covered stick
c   The cast is finally trimmed with a wire loop

40   Cross section of shallow press mould with foot. After the clay slab has been pressed into the mould in the usual way additional clay is applied to produce a smooth curved interior form

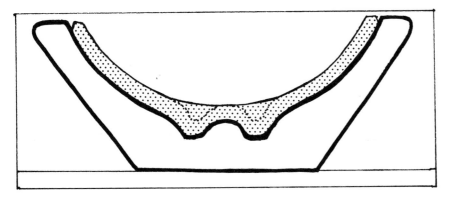

The methods described above are some of the most well known methods of achieving casts from one piece hollow and hump press moulds. However, there are a vast number of variations and experimental methods loosely based on these traditional ways, that open up many possibilities. The mould can be smeared with very thin applications of plastic or very soft 'buttery' clay to produce thin very fragile uneven edged forms. Layers of clay can be pressed into a mould in small units, pellets, thin plates, cut or rolled strips and layers or inlays of different textured or coloured clays. Try *not* pressing the clay slab against the sides of the mould, *not* rolling out a slab of an even thickness and *not* using a homogeneous clay. A mould can be filled with stiff and hard pieces of clay before pressing a plastic slab of clay into it. These dry pieces can be left on the surface of the cast, or they can be removed to produce indentations or thinner areas.

Be experimental, break so-called 'rules', learn from your 'failures', and remember what is considered 'wrong' in one context may be the most satisfactory way of expressing an idea in another. For example, different textured, types and coloured clays have different shrinkage rates and if they are combined in a mould they will either separate or cracks will appear in the cast. This method may express an idea far more efficiently than making a cast in the traditional way, inlaying and applying coloured slips and textures and then simulating cracks and gaps by cutting and carving into it. In the first method, the materials, the process and the idea are linked in a far more coherent way.

TAKING A CAST FROM A TWO PIECE PRESS MOULD

Before dealing with the making of a cast from a two piece press mould remember that a three dimensional clay form can also be formed by taking two casts from a hollow or hump press mould and joining their edges together. This is done by taking a cast from the press mould in the way already described, making certain that the top edge of it is level with the mould. Leave the cast to stiffen slightly (normally 10–15 minutes), place a rigid board (at least 50–76 mm (2–3 in.) larger than the cast) over the mould and carefully invert both mould and board. Once upside down carefully remove the mould, leaving the cast resting on the board. See figures 41a and b. Run a finger or rounded modelling tool around the cast sealing the clay to the board. The air trapped between the clay and board should prevent the clay from flopping and distorting. Cover this first cast with polythene to keep it damp until needed. Make another cast in the same mould, again carefully trimming the top edge level with the mould and *leave this second cast in the mould.* Apply slip to the edges that are to be joined and attach the first cast to the second, carefully sealing the edges on the outside with extra rolls of clay and working them across the joins. See figure 42a. To give extra strength sometimes a roll of clay can be partially smoothed into the inside edge of the second cast before the first is placed over it.

41   Cross sections of the stages in the removal of a cast from a press mould
a   When the cast has been taken and has dried slightly, a rigid board is placed over the mould and both are inverted
b   The mould is carefully removed leaving the cast on the board

a

b

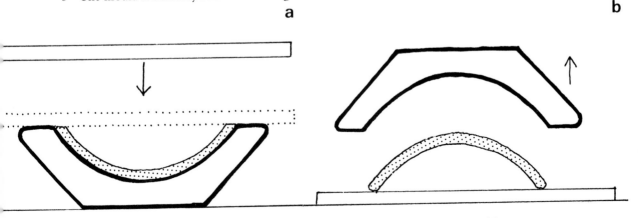

When the casts are stiffer and a hole has been made in the form a rounded stick can be used to smooth the rest of the clay roll into the join. See figure 42b. The joining of the two pieces should be done as quickly as possible after the second cast has been made, so that they do not dry out too much. Remember it is best that pieces of clay that are being joined should be of the same plasticity. Do not pierce the hollow form until it is stiffer and able to support itself, until then the trapped air will provide this. If the top cast starts to sag it is possible to insert a straw and inflate the form. Make certain a hole is made for the air to escape before the object is fired.

42   Cross sections showing the joining of two casts
a   The first cast is placed on the second which is left in the mould. Rolls of clay are applied to the inner and outer edges before the two pieces are joined
b   When the assembled pieces are stiffer, a hole is cut and with a piece of foam rubber on a stick smooth the rolls of clay into the joins

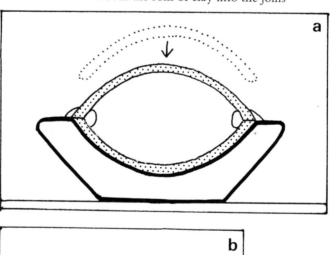

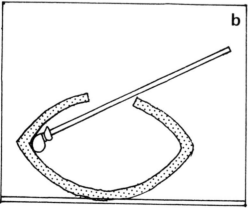

When press moulding from a two piece mould, the two pieces are filled individually in the way already described, but the clay is trimmed slightly higher, leaving about 6–12 mm ($\frac{1}{4}$–$\frac{1}{2}$ in.) projecting higher than the moulds. These edges are then coated with slip and the two halves are brought together, using the keys to locate them. See figure 43. The two halves are pressed firmly together until the outsides of the moulds almost meet. The excess clay squeezed between the two pieces always prevents them meeting completely. This is why some people prefer a two piece press mould to contain a spare, which is a channel for excess clay to be pushed into during pressing. See figure 44. After locating the two pieces and pressing them together firmly leave to harden and slightly stiffen before trimming off any surplus clay, seams, or spare on the outside surface and if this is possible smoothing the internal surface where the two pieces join.

43 Cross sections showing the stages in taking a cast from a two piece mould that has no spare

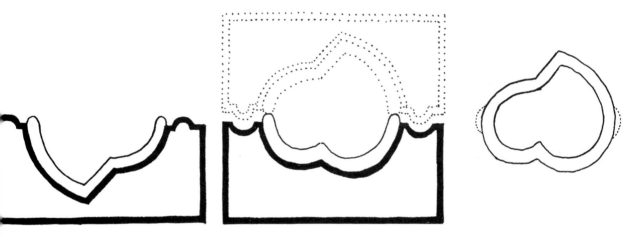

44 Cross sections showing the stages in taking a cast from a two piece mould with a spare

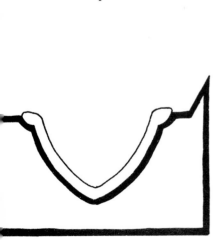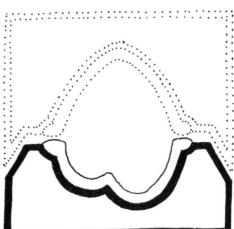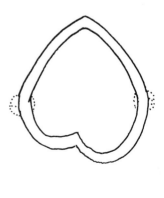

DEVELOPMENTS FROM PRESS MOULDED FORMS

Throughout this book moulded and slip cast forms are considered primarily as sub-structures or forms not complete in their own right apart from fettling, decorative treatments or firings. They need to be modified or developed by other processes and techniques like coiling, slabbing, throwing, pinching and modelling, have additions of other press moulded or slip cast units, or be rearranged or reorganised in form from their original shape. Press moulded or slip cast forms as described in this book can be modified in numerous ways before they are bisque fired.

Carving, cutting and incising can be done as soon as the object has been press moulded or slip cast and any seams fettled, providing it is firm enough to retain its shape. However, the quality of the cut or carving will depend on the condition as well as the type of clay, and the tool being used. If the clay is very soft 'ragged and rough' cuts occur as the knife drags on the clay, while if the clay is hard and brittle there will be 'ragged and rough' cuts of a very different quality. If the clay is leather hard, rather like the consistency of cheese, clean, sharp and more controllable cuts are possible.

There are a great number and variety of ways in which such forms can be treated: decorative cuts or carvings on the surface or incisions completely through the cast form; parts of a cast cut away and the pieces discarded or fixed to other parts of the same form; cast forms cut into a number of pieces or sections and reassembled into a completely different form. Remember to always use a mask when scraping, sanding, or carving into dry clay as the risk of silicosis is a very real one if you breathe in clay dust.

Pinching, squeezing and distorting will produce forms that will vary greatly with the plasticity and the type of clay and the quality and amount of pressure being used. These ways of modifying press moulded and slip cast forms are particularly suitable for a sequential development of a number of forms – a form moving through a series of changes or modifications – the metamorphosis of a form.

Press moulded in fabric, stoneware form
with suede addition. Pat Kongable, student
Barry Summer School

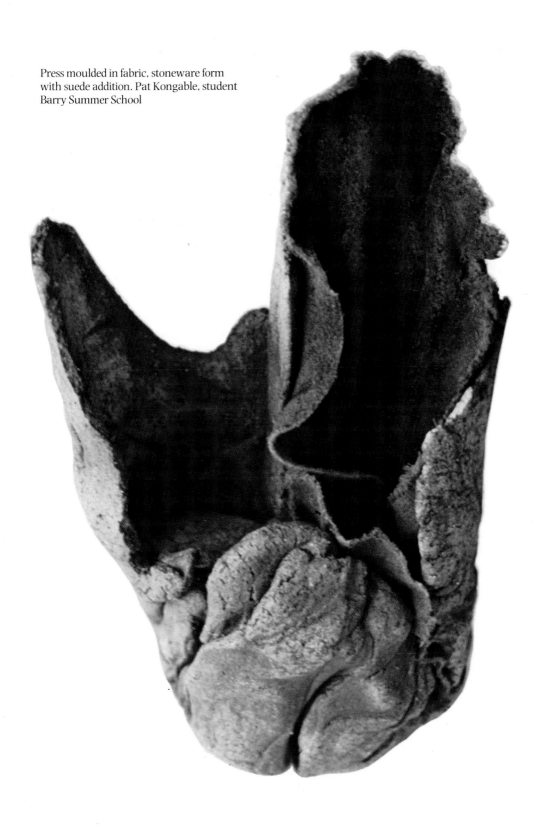

Assemblage of press moulded porcelain, stoneware, earthenware and raku casts
from student's hand and face. Student, Barry Summer School

Press moulded slab constructions. Stoneware and porcelain. Leisal Lawrence

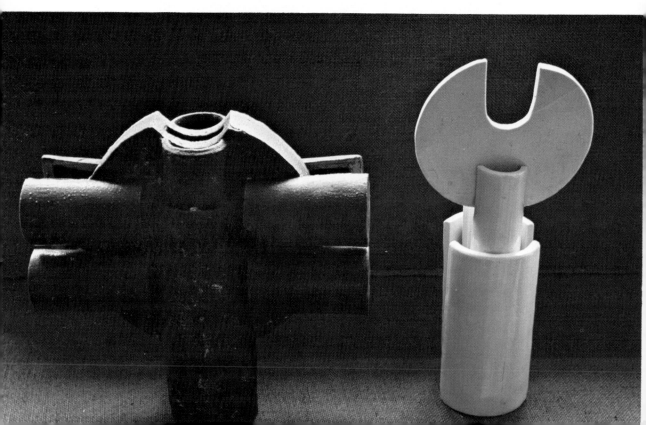

Joining Press moulded forms can either be joined or assembled in their plastic or leather hard states with slip, or after all firing and decorative processes have been completed with araldite, any epoxy resin, or similarly strong adhesive.

Casts being joined in their plastic state must be of the same plasticity when they are being assembled. This needs careful realization of their strength and plasticity – if the clay is too dry, or one piece is more plastic than another, they will not bond together, while if the clay is too wet the forms will loose their shape. Sometimes part of a joined form which needs to be kept quite damp can be supported in the mould. Another way is to plan the interlocking of the moulded forms being used, rather than physically joining or welding them together. This method has the added interest of assembling these interlocking forms, especially if there is more than one way, or different permutations, in which the individual units can be assembled.

The partial moulding of a form is particularly useful when a constructional problem is involved. For example, a form that comes out sharply from a small narrow base, is difficult to construct totally from coils. However, a base can be made in a press mould and the remainder coiled. The mould contains and supports the base until it is dry enough to take the total weight and support itself. See figure 45.

Apart from helping to overcome such obvious constructional problems partial moulding can make a more positive contribution to the expressive statement of the work. For example the statement may involve contrasting possible fluid qualities of freely wheel thrown clay with the more formal qualities of multiple castings or mouldings.

All these processes should be looked upon merely as 'jumping off' points. Use them as a basis for experimentation, rather than following them slavishly. Learn from so-called failures, remembering a failure in one piece may be just the quality you want in another. Try and experiment within an idea, set yourself a limit, yet be aware of other possibilities as you work. Unstructured experimentation can often be fruitless and self-indulgent, unless linked however tenuously, to an aim, purpose or idea. The plates that follow show a variety of forms and ideas that can be achieved by press moulding, by itself or in conjunction with other ceramic techniques and processes.

45   Eltham Green School

46   Penny Gregory, student

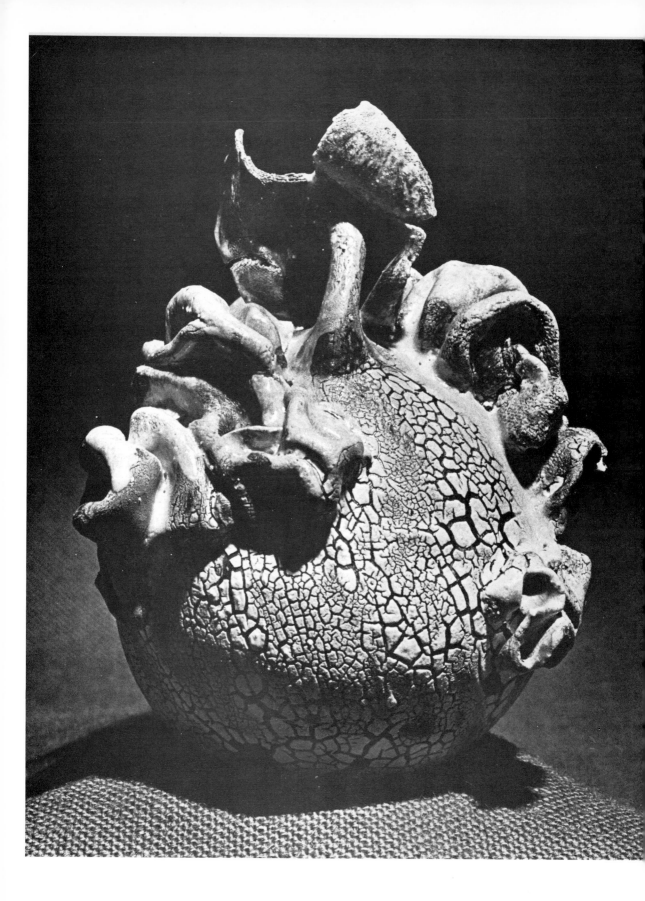

47   Barbara McPherson, student

48   Barbara McPherson, student

49   Barbara McPherson, student

50   Linda Peppit, student

51   Linda Peppit, student

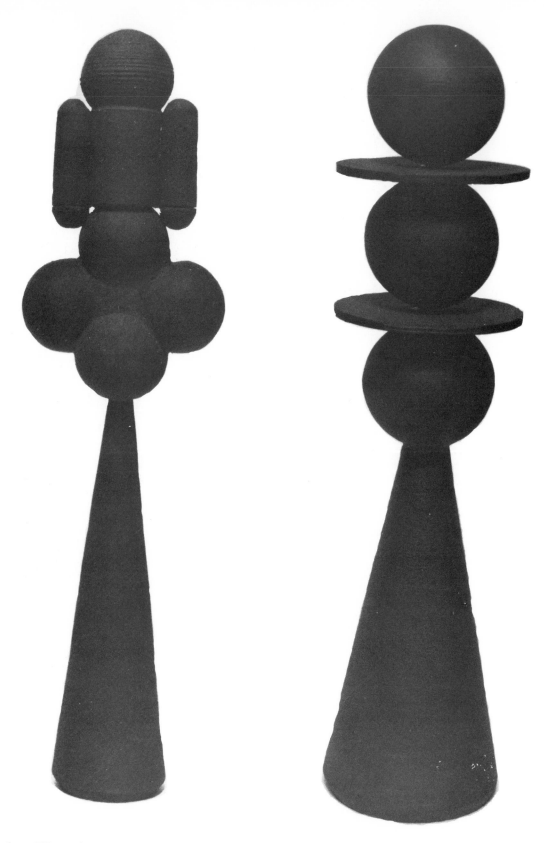

52 Graham Silk, student

53 Graham Silk, student

54 Graham Silk, student

55 Graham Silk, student

56   Graham Silk, student

57   Vivienne Bender, aged 16, Mayfield School

58 Janet Bartholomew, student

60 Jan Jackman, student

61 Margaret Backhouse, student

62 Clay and fabric construction, student, Barry Summer School

63   Maureen White, student, Froebel Institute

64   Jyl Fountain

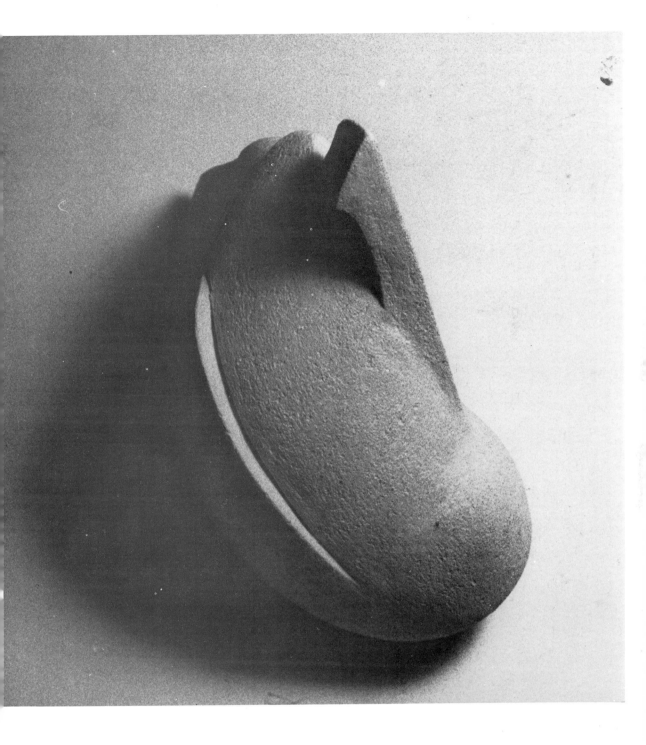

65   Jyl Fountain

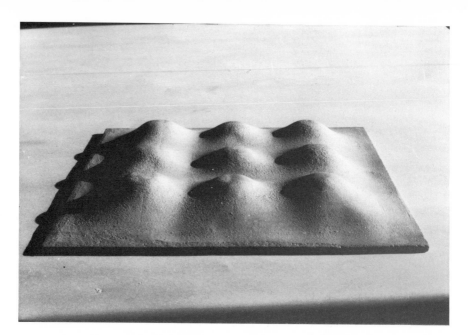

66 and 67　Relief, press moulded from apple tray, students' work

68 Modular relief with moveable units, students' work

69   Diana Dixon, student

70 and 71   Forms press moulded from hands, students' work

72   Elizabeth McFarlane, student

73   Graham Silk, student

74 Press moulded and slip cast form from the same mould

Slip Cast Ceramics

As in press moulding the shape of the object is determined by a mould. However, in this case liquid clay or casting slip is used to produce the cast, instead of plastic clay. The basic principle is that casting slip, a liquid clay made from mixing dry clay, water and deflocculants in certain proportions, is poured into a mould made from an absorbent material, usually plaster of paris. This mould absorbs a high proportion of water from the casting slip and a layer of stiff clay is gradually formed on the inside of the mould. The thickness of this layer will depend upon

70

the time the casting slip is left in the mould. When it is of the required thickness, the excess casting slip is poured off. As the clay in the mould dries, it shrinks and pulls away from the sides of the mould. As soon as this cast or shell of clay has loosened itself completely from the mould and is still plastic enough yet firm enough to retain its shape when handled, it is removed from the mould and forming marks or seams are smoothed or fettled, any additions made and the form is finally allowed to dry slowly and evenly before the bisque firing.

Before the use of slip casting techniques were developed, clay positives made separately in press moulds and joined together to achieve a three dimensional form, were widely used, though they were never totally satisfactory because of the roughness of the seams or joins. Pieces were often 'worked up' later but this meant extra work. Slip casting made possible elaborate and complex multiple piece moulds, producing castings such as the porcelain figures made in European factories at Meissen and Nymphenburg. However, it was only with the development of deflocculants in the late nineteenth century that slip casting superseded press moulding as the most efficient and economical method of mass production in ceramics. Before this, vast amounts of water needed to be absorbed by a mould, which wore them out too quickly for them to be economical.

Slip casting can involve much complicated chemistry which is outside the scope of this introduction. However, it is essential to understand even at a very simple level the importance and place of deflocculants in the process of slip casting. Before deflocculants were used slip, clay mixed with water to a pourable consistency was used to take casts. The two great disadvantages of using this slip was firstly the amount of water absorbed by the mould was considerable during each casting, so the saturated mould had to be dried between each casting. Secondly, the high shrinkage of the cast. The problem, therefore, was to reduce the water content of the slip while still retaining its fluidity. The discovery that sodium silicate added to a slip made it possible to reduce to as little as 25% the water needed in a slip of the same fluidity. Sodium silicate and other chemicals that produce the same results are known as deflocculants. High shrinkage and mould wear still effect the ceramic casting industry but deflocculants certainly lessened them, making slip casting the viable process in mass production it is today.

Though slip casting has been associated with the manufacture of domestic tableware, sanitary ware and highly regulated technical and industrial ceramics, rather than the individual creative artist making a personal statement, more and more people working in clay today are finding that this process lends itself admirably to the expression of their ideas.

Moulds for slip casting can be made from any absorbent material like bisque fired clay, paper, cardboard and fabrics, though the most efficient and widely used are those that are made from plaster of paris.

The basic principles are obviously much the same as those that apply to press moulds, in fact, slip casts can easily be taken from press moulds, with the advantage of the casts being much thinner and finer, as well as picking up much finer detail from the mould than if they were press moulded. However, if a two or more piece press mould is to be used, a channel must be made through which the casting slip can be poured and removed. Slip cast moulds can be much deeper than press moulds but again must obviously not have any undercutting. Press moulds are usually shallow, so that plastic slab clay can be easily pressed into them without cracking or tearing. With slip casting this is not a problem, though with a very deep mould be careful not to trap air in the mould as casting slip is poured in.

Moulds that are being made specifically for slip casting can be made from a model in any material providing it will retain its shape when the plaster of paris is poured over it. However, the most widely used models are those that have been made of plaster of paris as they tend to give the smoothest surface.

Symmetrical models made in plaster of paris can be turned on a power driven lathe or wheel, though if such machinery is not available they can be made by using a turning box or the equipment shown in figures 75, 76 and 77. Assymetrical forms for models can be freely modelled in plaster of paris or clay and 'found' objects in metal, wood, plastic, rubber or glass can often make excellent models for moulds. When choosing or making models bear in mind the fundamental principles of undercutting and try to keep the number of pieces that make up the mould to a minimum.

Slip cast relief. David Cowley

Press moulded in fabric, raku form. Student

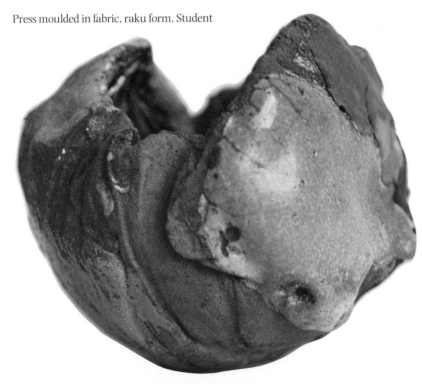

(Overleaf) Removing a cast from a two piece mould

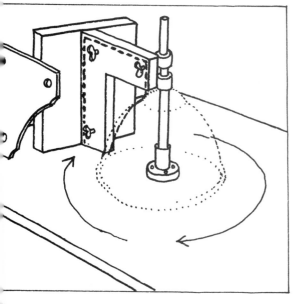

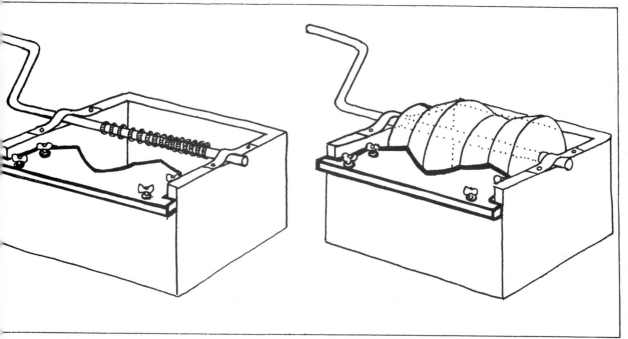

75 A rotating template or jack shapes the wet plaster that is slowly built up
around the spindle. A removable template makes it possible to create a variety of
plaster models

76 A turning lathe, on which plaster models can be made, is available from
pottery suppliers

77 An easily made turning box. Wet plaster is applied to the rod as it rotates.
The plaster form is determined by the removable template

MAKING A ONE PIECE PLASTER
SLIP CAST MOULD

1   The model is turned in plaster of paris or clay upside down on a wheel, the form extending outwards 12 mm ($\frac{1}{2}$ in.) onto the wheel, to create a spare. See figure 78a.

2   The model is smoothed and polished and a separator is applied, if needed, to all surface to be covered with plaster of paris. A cottle is made from stiff cardboard or lino, placed around the model, tied firmly and all seams filled from the inside, before the plaster of paris is poured over the model. See figure 78b.

3   When the plaster of paris has set, it is separated from the wheel, and the model carefully removed. See figure 78c. All outside edges of the mould are bevelled and smoothed and the mould is left to dry evenly and thoroughly before being used. See figure 78d.

A one piece mould can either be made by pouring the plaster of paris over the model or the model can be carefully pressed into liquid plaster of paris that is just beginning to set, contained within a cottle. The 'found' object made of plastic has to be weighted with clay to prevent it floating when plaster of paris is poured over it.

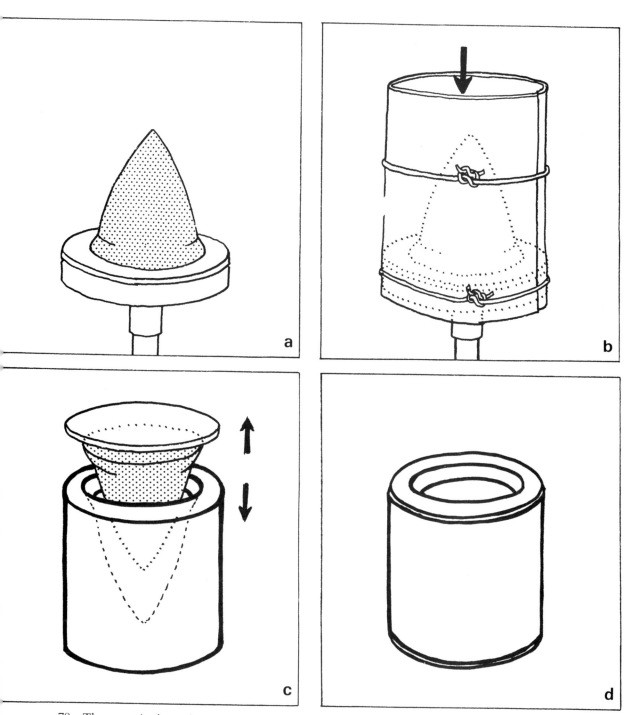

78 The stages in the making of a simple one piece plaster slip cast mould

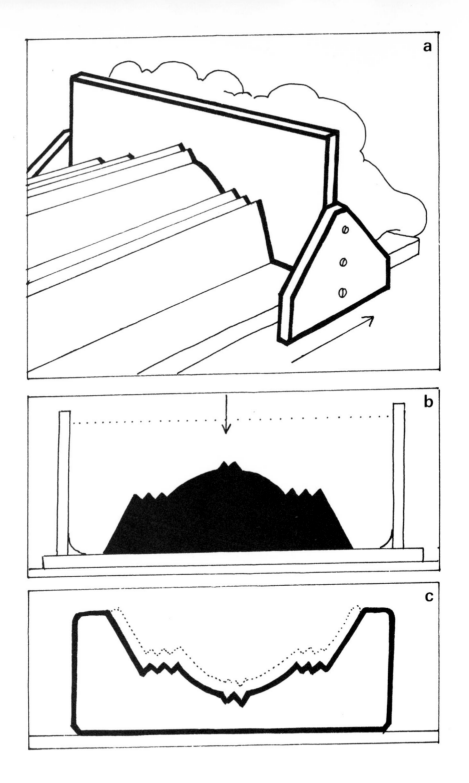

79   A model can also be made by a process very similar to that used to make plaster mouldings. A template or jack is dragged through soft plaster. Curved as well as straight forms can be made in this way
a   The jack is made to fit over the edge of a table, which holds it firmly as it is repeatedly dragged through the plaster
b   Plaster is poured over this model to create the mould, after applying a separator
c   The finished mould ready for casting

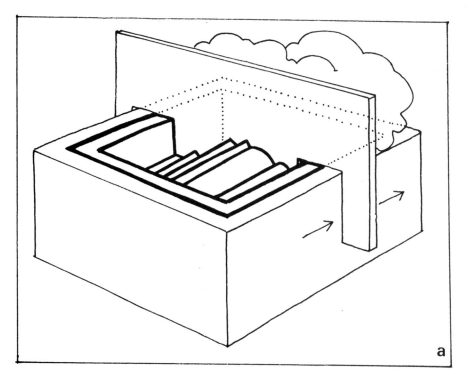

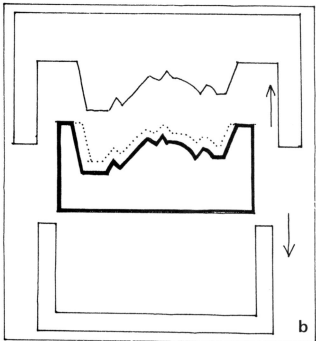

80 *a* A quicker method is to fill a casting box with plaster and while it is still soft a jack is dragged into and through it. It is very important to leave a wall of plaster all the way round the hollow form
b The separated plaster mould template or jack and the casting box

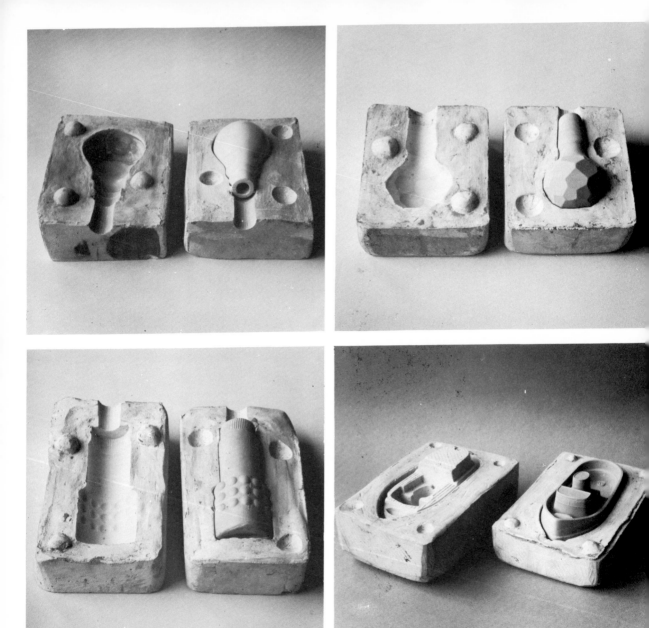

81 to 84   Two piece moulds taken from found objects, students' work

85   Cross section of the stages in the making of a two piece plaster mould from
a sphere
a   Sphere resting on clay pad is covered with clay up to its parting seam
b   A cottle is placed around the clay bed and plaster is poured up to level (A)

MAKING A TWO PIECE PLASTER SLIP CAST MOULD

The procedure is much the same as that described earlier for the making of a two piece plaster press mould, except in this case a channel through which the mould is filled and emptied has to be made. This section shows how to make a simple two piece mould for a sphere from a rubber ball.

1   Firstly, find the parting line or seam on the model as previously described. However, in this case the original rubber casting seam on the ball can be clearly seen. This is the great advantage of using previously cast 'found' objects.

2   Place the ball on a pad or cushion of clay with the seam horizontal to the working surface. The whole thing should rest on a rigid board at least 50–76 mm (2–3 in.) larger than the model. With this mould a throwing bat (50 mm (2 in.) larger than the diameter of the ball was used. Build up plastic clay carefully around the ball, until it is level with the seam and make certain that the clay extends horizontally from the ball. Smooth the top surface of this clay bed. See figure 85a.

3   Coat the model with a separator if this is necessary. In this case it was not necessary because rubber and plaster of paris do not adhere to one another. Place a wall or cottle around the clay bed, this should be about 38–50 mm (1½–2 in.) from the seam of the ball and at least 2–3 in. higher than the highest part of the ball. Mark a line on the inside of the cottle up to which the liquid plaster of paris will be poured, about 38–50 mm (1½–2 in.) from the highest part of the model. Seal all the gaps from the inside through which the liquid plaster of paris may escape. See figure 85b.

4   Mix the plaster of paris and pour it carefully into the cottle until it covers the exposed half of the model, or ball, and reaches the mark previously made. Avoid trapping air as you pour, tapping the sides of the cottle to bring any air to the surface. Let the plaster set, which usually takes about 20–30 minutes.

85

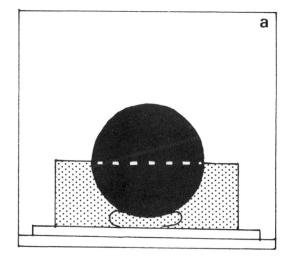
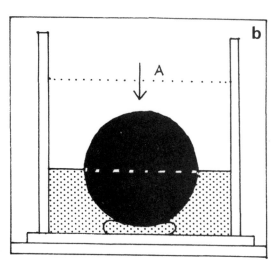

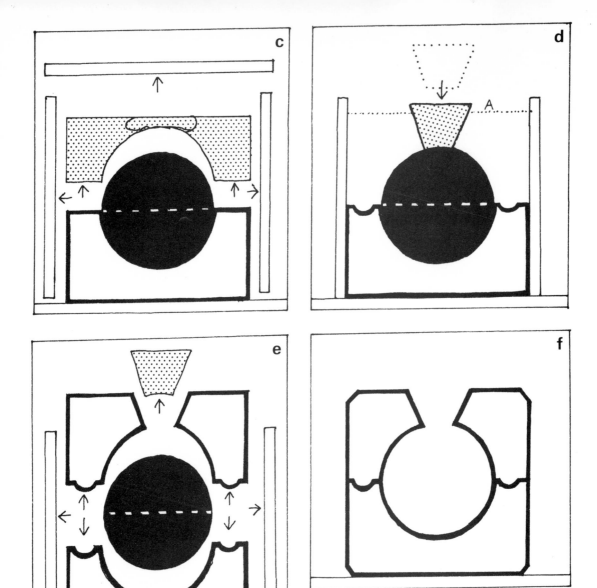

85 *continued*
c Remove the cottle, invert the block so that the plaster is now resting on the work surface, and remove the clay bed
d Kays are cut, cottle is replaced, clay plug is placed on sphere, separator is applied and plaster is poured in to level (A)
e Separated moulds, sphere, cottle and clay plug
f Reassembled, surformed and dried mould ready for slip casting

5   When the plaster of paris has set, invert the whole thing so that the plaster of paris is now resting on the work surface. Remove the board or bat and the clay but be very careful not to separate the model from the plaster of paris. See figure 85c. Cut keys in the top surface of the plaster and add the inverted clay cone about 50 mm (2 in.) high to the top of the model. This will eventually form the channel through which the casting slip will be poured. Coat the surface of the plaster with a separator (the clay and rubber surfaces do not need treating), replace the cottle, seal, and pour in the plaster of paris until it reaches the top of the inverted clay cone, but does not cover it. See figure 85d.
6   When the plaster has set, remove the cottle, the clay cone, any seams and carefully separate the two pieces of the mould. Remove the model and wash away all traces of clay and separator with a very soft brush. See figure 85e. Relocate the two pieces, hold them together with rubber bands, bevel and soften the outside edges of the mould. Allow to dry evenly and slowly, figure 85f.

Sometimes the spare used as the pouring channel is formed in a separate mould piece, rather than as part of the second piece of the mould as just described. So the spare is made by adding the plug of clay to the model before the second pouring or before the third pouring, depending whether it is the second piece of the mould or separate and in the third piece. See figure 86.

86   Spare contained within one piece of mould
      Spare contained within separate piece of mould

The spare is important because as the water from the casting slip is absorbed by the plaster mould, the level of the casting slip naturally falls and needs to be topped up. To avoid frequent additions of casting slip during a casting, the spare serves as a reservoir as well as a funnel for the slip. It also acts as a guide in the trimming of the top edge of the cast. It is very important not to make the pouring channel too narrow as during casting the slip may block it and prevent the excess from being removed. See figures 87a and b.

Two piece moulds can also be used to determine different inside and outside profiles of a form as shown by figures 87c and d.

Two piece moulds can also be used to produce solid castings. These are different from the castings already mentioned, sometimes known as drain castings, in that solid castings are taken from a mould that shapes the inside as well as the outside of the form. So in many castings taken from a mould, the thicknesses of each piece are identical and not as in drain moulds dependent upon the time the casting slip is left in the mould. The advantage of solid casting is that a mould can be made to accommodate a variety of thickness within one single cast form, so the inside profile can be different from the outside. See figure 88.

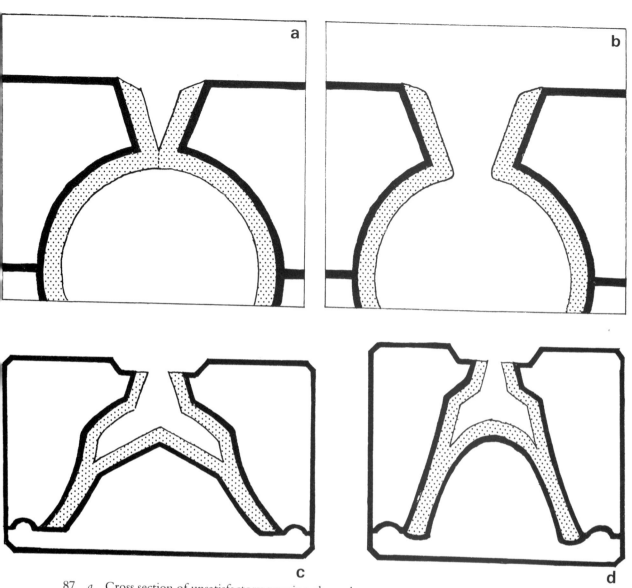

87   *a*   Cross section of unsatisfactory pouring channel
      b   Cross section of efficient pouring channel
c and *d*   Two piece moulds used to determine inside and outside profiles

88   *a*   Cross section of unsatisfactory interior form from a drain mould.
      b   Cross section from solid cast mould, having the same foot yet a more
         satisfactory interior form

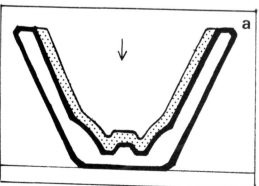

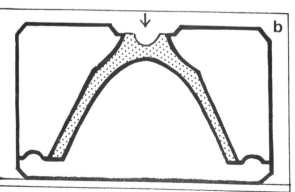

MAKING A TWO PIECE PLASTER
SOLID CAST SLIP MOULD

The mould is usually made from a rigid model preferably a bisque, and sometimes a glazed form. This model in this case a bowl is imbedded into a lump of clay up to its top rim and after a cottle is placed around and a separator is applied, plaster of paris is poured into the interior form and about 38–50 mm (1½–2 in.) above the rim. See figure 89a.

When the plaster has set, the whole thing is inverted and the clay bed is removed. Keys are cut in the plaster, the clay plug is fixed to the model, the cottle is replaced and the separator is applied. The plaster of paris is poured over the outside of the model and about 38–50 mm (1½–2 in.) above the highest point of the model. See figure 89b.

Remove the clay plug when the plaster has set. The two pieces of the mould are carefully separated, the model is removed and all surfaces are carefully cleaned before leaving the cast to dry thoroughly. See figures 89c and d.

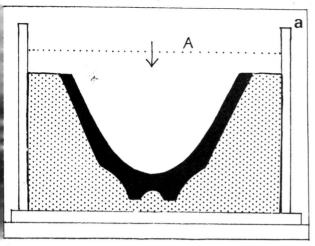
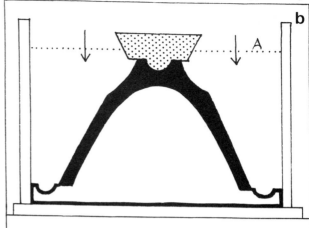
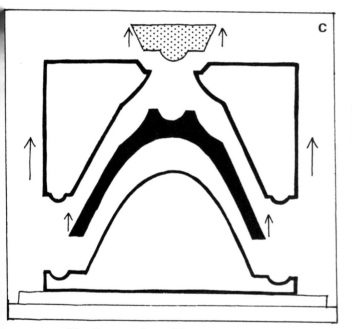
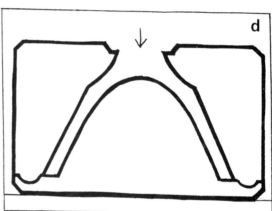

89 Cross section of the stages in the making of a two piece solid cast plaster mould

a Model is imbedded in clay. Liquid plaster is poured up to level (A) when the cottle has been fixed

b Inverted model and plaster with clay bed removed. Keys are cut, plug is placed on model, separator is applied, and plaster is poured up to level (A)

c Separated mould pieces, model and clay plug

d Reassembled, bevelled, and dried mould ready for casting

MULTIPLE PIECE PLASTER MOULDS

The making of a multiple piece plaster of paris mould can be a very complicated process and should not be attempted before the basic principles of simple one and two piece moulds has been thoroughly understood. However, the following brief guide lines may be helpful to those of you attempting such a mould. Carefully examine the model to see how many pieces will be required and where the seams are likely to occur. Seams nearly always show on a cast, even after careful fettling, so if possible they should occur along obvious changes of form or natural divisions. The pieces of the mould must be planned so that sections can be removed without damage to keys or subsequent casts. The order in which the pieces of the mould are separated from the cast is very important and needs careful thought. Also the usual half-spherical depression keys may not always be a good idea, especially if a mould needs to be withdrawn in a particular direction. Badly placed and directioned keys may lock the pieces of the mould together, making withdrawal impossible without destroying the cast. Keys placed on the outside edge of a mould, or corner keys may be more satisfactory for multiple piece moulds, making withdrawal of mould pieces much easier. See figures 90a and b. Another thing to bear in mind is that sections of a multiple piece mould need to be of different sizes, smaller pieces being held together by larger ones. If all sections are of the same size, rubber bands or clamps may cause the pieces of the mould to fly apart.

90

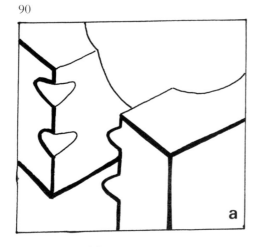
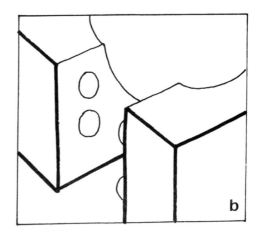

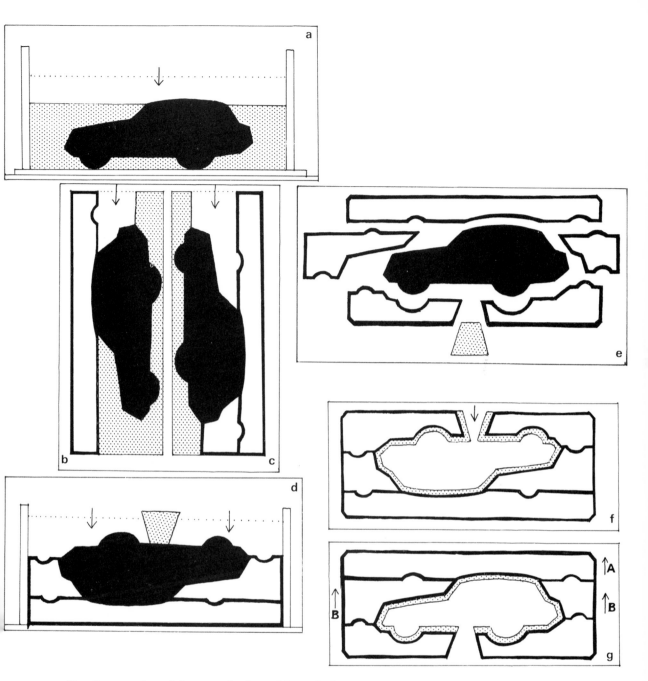

91 Cross section of the stages in the making of a four piece mould from a toy car. See plate 122, page 115

a After deciding on the position of seams and mould sections, the model is imbedded in clay, with one section of the model revealed. Plaster is poured over this when a cottle has been fixed

b The block is turned over, through 90°, clay is removed to reveal another section, which is covered with plaster when keys have been cut and a separator has been applied

c Another section is revealed and covered with plaster

d Before pouring in the final layer of plaster a clay plug is fixed to the model to act as a pouring channel and the spare

e The separated pieces of the mould, model and the clay plug

f The reassembled mould with cast prior to trimming of the spare

g The spare is trimmed, the mould is inverted, and the pieces are separated carefully. Important to remember that the mould pieces should be separated in a particular order

MOULDS FROM OTHER MATERIALS

Any material which will absorb the water content of a casting slip relatively quickly will function as a mould. Sand, paper, fabric and cardboard will often function well as moulding agents. Though the successful use of these will depend upon how much experimentation you are willing to do in discovering the most appropriate material for your particular idea. The great variety of forms and surfaces that can be achieved are excitingly full of possibilities, provided you do not expect the qualities normally associated with the traditional slip cast. These experimental moulds can provide exciting linkages between idea, material and process in a dynamic and positive way.

Slip casts from fabrics

The most satisfactory results seem to be achieved from open weave, thin fabric. So although the fabric determines the shape of the cast, it is the atmosphere that is the drying agent. A source of heated air, perhaps from a hair dryer, can also be used to dry the casting slip. Fabrics that have a high absorbency can be equally satisfactory. However, experiment with a variety of fabrics and discover the particular forms and surfaces that can be achieved.

These types of moulds can take the form of slings, fabric slung between the legs of an upturned stool, crumpled and folded fabric, fabric laid into a simple one piece mould before pouring casting slip into it, or bag or container forms that are filled and empties with casting slip through a funnel.

The separation of the solidified casting slip from the fabric needs to be done when the slip is stiff enough to retain its shape but pliable enough to remove the fabric without cracking the clay. Woven or knitted fabrics can be dipped in casting slip and moulded by laying them over cardboard forms, inflated balloons, or any form that modifies them, being removed when the casting slip has stiffened and solidified.

Slip casts from paper and cardboard

Much of the moulded and compressed paper or cardboard used in display and packaging can provide ready made moulds for casting slip. Corrugated cardboard and vegetable or fruit containers are particularly suitable. The insides of plaster of paris moulds and shallow trays of cardboard can be modified by the application of absorbent paper or cardboard cut or torn pieces, laid in before or after the casting slip is poured in. This can produce shallow reliefs of great delicacy and subtlety.

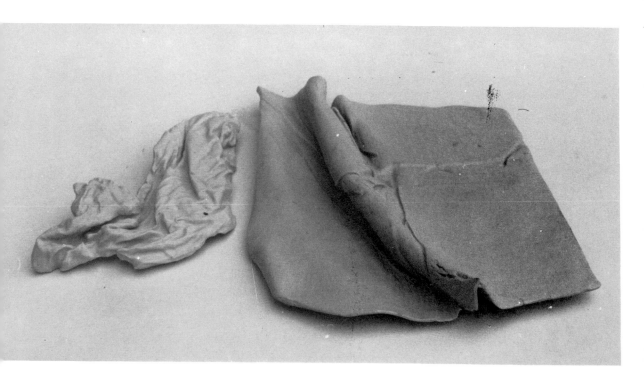

92 and 93   Slip casts from fabrics, students' work Barry Summer School

Slip casts from sand

The sand can either be dry or damp enough to form a bond between the particles. This depends upon the quality and definition wanted from this type of mould. However, it is always better to work within a wooden box or rigid container. The forms within this box can be freely modelled, carved, or formed in any way, remembering, however, that all hollows will cast as raised forms and vice versa.

Damp sand should be used to reproduce a model. The model can be pressed into a box filled with sand, which then should be firmly pressed against the model before it is removed. The model can also be placed face upwards on a rigid board, a firm box without a base or lid is placed around the object which is then filled with damp sand. This is firmly pressed or stamped down, making certain that the sand is level with the top of the box. Place a rigid board over the top and invert the whole thing. Remove the board that is now on top and carefully remove the model from the sand. If the model has any undercutting it will displace some sand as it is removed, ruining this mould, so choose a model carefully.

Casting slip is poured into the sand being very careful not to displace any as you pour. Sometimes pouring into a spoon held slightly above the sand, rather than pouring directly into the sand helps to prevent this displacement. The casting slip may take some time to dry and achieve the required thickness, but when this is done, the excess slip can be carefully spooned out, absorbed with a sponge, or a plug of dry plaster of paris can be placed into the centre of the well of casting slip to absorb the excess. Leave the cast until it is leather hard, then place a rigid board over it, invert and carefully remove the sand with a very soft brush.

The disadvantage of this method of casting is that the mould is destroyed with each casting. However, in terms of surface qualities and directness of process, it has much to recommend it.

CASTING SLIP

Clay mixed with water will produce slip but for the reasons already mentioned such a *water slip* is not the most satisfactory material from which to obtain a good cast. Such water slips may sometimes be satisfactory for a simple one piece drain mould but the tendency for them to settle, their high shrinkage, warpage and the tendency to crack in the mould, makes them unsatisfactory for more complex ones.

Water slips of a fluid, pouring consistency are usually made from equal parts of water and clay, while a *casting slip, or deflocculated clay* may contain as little as a quarter of its weight as water, and yet still be of a fluid pourable consistency. The latter naturally has the great advantages of low shrinkage from wet to dry states and a low saturation of moulds.

Deflocculation   Individual clay particles have a static electrical charge which makes them stick, draw together in groups or *flock*. So in order to make a clay fluid, the particles have to be separated from one another, or dispersed, in other words, break up the flock. This can be done by adding a great deal of water to make them a liquid suspension, or by adding to a clay a substance known as an *electrolyte*. An electrolyte usually an alkali, such as *sodium silicate* or *soda ash*, changes the electrical charge on the clay particles, which now repel one another and float individually rather than flocking together. The clay is now said to be de-flocculated. Try a simple test which shows how the addition of deflocculants will considerably reduce the amount of water needed to make it fluid. Mix a 1000 g of dry clay with 400 g of water (35 oz of dry clay with 14 oz of water) and then add a few drops of sodium silicate. The sticky mass of clay and water will soon alter from that state to a smooth, pourable and creamy liquid with the addition of the sodium silicate. However, if it becomes liquid then quickly jells, too much electrolyte or deflocculant has been added. Only a very small amount is necessary, usually about 0·3%–0·5% of the weight of the clay being used. This simple test will not work for all clays, some do not deflocculate and others require the addition of both sodium silicate and soda ash.

The good casting slip needs to maintain clay particles in suspension, produce good definition from a mould, shrink as little as possible, have a good strength when dry, and not excessively saturate the mould.

Alkalis like sodium silicate and soda ash are corrosive and after about 20–30 casts a plaster of paris mould will lose its definition, so it is always important to keep the model so that other moulds can be made from it. Also after some time a fungus-like growth will occur on moulds, which is due to the absorption by the mould of some of the electrolytes from the deflocculated slip.

Casting slip is nearly always thought of as being fine, smooth and white, mainly because of the extensive use of such bodies in the ceramic industry. However, there is no reason why casting slips should not be coloured with metal oxides to produce a whole range of colours, or grogged for a variety of textures and have the whole firing range, earthenware, stoneware and porcelain. In fact the whole range of colour, texture and firing temperatures is possible.

Mixing a casting slip

Generally casting slips contain for every 100 parts by weight of clay (and other ingredients like flint, feldspar and cornish stone) about 35–50 parts of water and less than 1 part of sodium silicate and soda ash. There are a number of recipes that are easily available and some are listed on page 93. It might be useful to mix and test these, and others, until you arrive at one that suits your work. The following guide lines may be useful.

Carefully weigh out all the ingredients, using powdered rather than plastic clay, as it is much easier to mix with water. The soda ash should be dissolved in hot or warm water taken from the total amount needed and then both deflocculants added to the rest of the water. Remember there are several grades of sodium silicate, measured in 'degrees of twaddle' (°TW) so use the correct one for the recipe. Mix the dry ingredients thoroughly together and gradually add this to the water, stirring continuously. A blunger or powered mixer certainly helps, though there is no reason why it cannot be done by hand. When thoroughly mixed the slip should be passed through a 60 mesh sieve and left for a day or two before being used. Always store in an airtight container and sieve before use.

There are other methods of mixing casting slip, though the above method is probably the easiest and the most efficient but however you mix a casting slip proceed slowly and methodically, weighing all the ingredients very accurately. Even so, a casting slip may require minor adjustments to the amount or even the type of deflocculant, increasing or reducing the water content, altering the amounts and types of the dry ingredients, and perhaps even using a different clay. This may take much careful testing over a period of time. However, the information and procedure above is only a basis or introduction to the making of casting slip. Further understanding of the complexities can be achieved by personal experimentation and further reading of the books listed in the bibliography. If the reader is unable or does not wish to devote time to either, prepared casting slips can be bought from most of the major ceramic suppliers. These casting slips are supplied in plastic containers and all they need is to be passed through a sieve before they are used.

Recipes for casting slips can be found in many ceramic books. Two particularly versatile bodies are listed here:

A Semi-porcelain – 1280°C	B Earthenware – 1100°C
34·02 kg (75 lbs) Semi-porcelain clay	40 Ball clay
9·87 kg (21 lb 12 ozs) Water	15 China clay
56·7 g (2 ozs) Sodium silicate (140° TW)	17 Cornish stone
56·7 g (2 ozs) Soda ash	28 Flint
	+0·25% Sodium silicate (140° TW)
	0·20% Soda ash
	30 Water

Colour in casting slips

The main colouring ingredients for casting slip, as for most clays and glazes are metallic oxides, which are affected by temperature, whether the firing is of an oxidizing or reducing atmosphere, whether the casting slip is finally glazed or not and obviously the amount of pigment being used.

Start by limiting yourself to a few basic oxides and add about 5% of the oxide to the casting slip. Test in oxidizing and reducing atmospheres and to start with two glazes, a transparent and an opaque. Having tested them do the necessary additions or subtractions of the oxides to achieve the colours that suit your work. These are only rough guide lines to the colours that can be achieved with oxides. Cobalt oxide – blues. Copper oxide – greens and reds. Iron oxide – yellows and browns. Manganese oxide – browns and blacks. Always mix the dry oxide with water to achieve good dispersal in the casting slip unless an uneven colour is required.

Texture in casting slips

Sawdust, fibres, sand, and wood shavings can be added to the casting slip. Some of these will burn away leaving hollows where they were originally, while others will provide a permanent texture to the body and can be emphasized by dragging a tool over or sanding the surface. Experiment with a wide variety of materials and scraps which are not normally associated with ceramic bodies.

The storage of casting slips

Always store casting slips in airtight plastic containers, preferably those with wide necks and screw top lids. Most slips will normally retain their properties over a long period, though if kept for too long fermentation can occur, causing pin holing in the casts. Sometimes a small addition of water restores the fluidity if the slip has become too solid but be careful of such additions until you are familiar with the properties of that particular slip. Usually sieving or a thorough mixing will return the casting slip to its fluid condition.

For the beginner a good rule is to keep the casting slip as 'pure' as possible. Any dried slip or scraps from spares should not be returned to the container, as the whole batch would then be ruined. Instead this waste should be kept separately and perhaps the more plastic pieces could be used for press moulding. There are ways of adjusting dry casting slip for use again but these can be difficult and very complicated for the beginner. Anyway such wastage can be minimal if you are careful and systematic in your approach to casting.

TAKING SLIP CASTS FROM PLASTER MOULDS

When using a plaster mould for the first time, the first few casts seldom prove to be successful. Satisfactory casts only come after two or three castings when the inside casting surface of the mould has received a slightly greasy, oily surface covering from the casting slip. This surface seems to help the easy separation of cast from mould, preventing sticking and subsequent cracks appearing, consequently it is important not to sponge the inside of a mould.

1   Make certain that the mould is clean and dry and if it is made up of more than one piece, that these pieces are firmly held together by thick rubber bands or clamps. Sections cut from the inner tube of a car tyre are often used for this purpose. See figure 95a.

2   Thoroughly mix and sieve the casting slip and pour into the mould in a smooth, steady stream. See figure 94. Pour into the bottom of the mould and avoid splashing or splattering the sides. If the mould has a narrow neck or pouring channel, use a funnel. If the rate of pouring is too slow and irregular, or the slip is too thick, horizontal lines or rings will appear on the outside surface of the cast.

3   As the plaster mould absorbs the moisture from the casting slip the level will drop and will need to be topped up with more slip. It is important to do this otherwise the cast may vary in thickness. Also there is no indication of the thickness of the cast lower in the mould.

4   The thickness of the cast will depend upon the viscosity of the slip and the absorbency of the mould as well as the length of time the slip is left in the mould. When the required thickness of slip is adhering to the sides of the mould, this can be seen by tilting the mould slightly or gently blowing into it, the mould is inverted and the excess is poured back into the container of casting slip. Be careful to invert the mould gradually, rotating it, to enable the slip to run out slowly as the air enters, otherwise a vacuum can suck in part of the cast. See figure 94b. This is most likely to happen with a narrow pouring channel. Keep the mould inverted for a few minutes, one side lower than the other, so that the excess slip can flow out. See figure 94c. This is important otherwise if the cast is righted too quickly the excess slip will run

94   Stages in the taking of a slip cast from a simple one piece drain mould
a   Filling the mould
b   Emptying the mould when the required thickness of cast has been achieved, turning the mould as this is done
c   Leaving the mould to drain thoroughly
d   Trimming the spare

back to the bottom, thickening the base and marking the inside surface. When inverting a mould be very careful that no pieces of dry slip, or chipped plaster from the mould fall into the container of casting slip.

5   Whenever possible the trimming of surplus slip should be done while the cast is still in the mould, helping to avoid distortion when trimming. Always trim towards the mould and not away from it. See figure 94d. Avoid cutting into the mould when this is done. Carefully choosing the right moment to trim the surplus obviously comes with experience but a guide can be when the cast has lost its surface sheen. If trimming is done too quickly the cast will distort, if left too late the piece will tear and perhaps crack.

6   The removal of the trimmed cast from the mould or separating the pieces of a multiple piece mould requires very careful judgement of when the cast is firm enough to retain its shape, has shrunk away from the sides of the mould and yet is plastic enough to take additions or alterations. Having separated the cast from the mould, scrape or fettle any seams or unwanted parts. Avoid excessive sponging, this is both unnecessary and it often destroys the character of the cast piece.

If the cast is still sticking after 3 or 4 castings have been taken, the slip is not dry enough, the ingredients need adjusting, or perhaps the mould has areas of undercutting locking the cast to it.

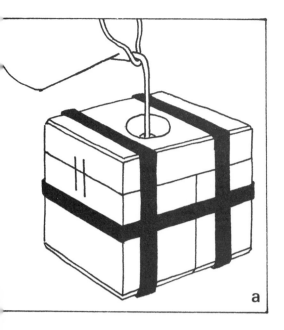

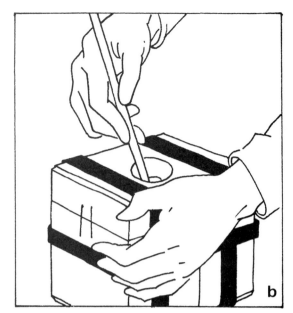

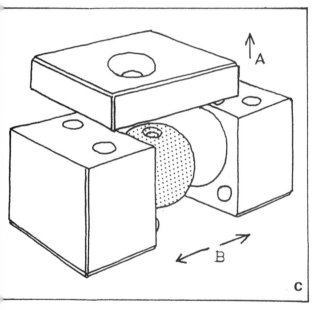

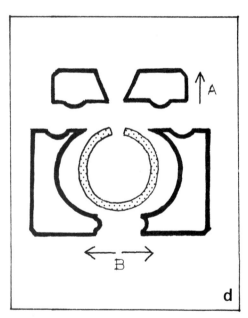

95 Stages in the taking of a cast from a three piece mould
a The mould is filled when the pieces are held together firmly with thick
rubber bands or sections cut from the inner tube of a car tyre
b Trimming the spare
c Separating the pieces of the mould from the cast
d Cross section showing the separation of pieces from cast

EXPERIMENTAL SLIP CASTS

The methods described earlier deal with the traditional ways of taking slip casts from plaster moulds and if done correctly these will produce casts of an even thickness, even shrinkage and little or no distortion during drying and firing. However, such standards that are required in highly regulated mass production, might not necessarily be those that are wanted by the individual artist. In fact the exploitation and development of so-called casting faults may provide just the means whereby he can make, and intensify, a creative and expressive personal statement. To take an example, the beginner casting a sphere, on inverting the mould too quickly, in order to pour out the excess slip, will discover that the vacuum formed sucks in a part of the cast. The relationship of this concave form on the sphere to its over-all convex form may with further development and experimentation become the basis of some creative work. These so-called 'mistakes' can be too quickly dismissed as having no creative possibilities. This is not a plea for shoddy workmanship, lack of standards, the loose structuring of work and work patterns, or the acceptance of the third rate or so-called 'happy accidents', but encouraging an open mind and an awareness of possibilities, even in the areas that we have been conditioned into believing as having none. We need to continually re-evaluate so-called rules in relation to our ideas. Obviously certain factual information needs to be learnt, but the real danger is that once this has been done it is considered as relevant in any context.

This section then deals with such experimental methods that break the rules of good casting. They are mainly suggestions on how to start your investigations. Try not just to copy the effects described or shown, but make your own discoveries. Be systematic and analytical.

1   Try pouring casting slip in thin streams onto the sides of the mould using a slip trailer with a narrow funnel. See figure 96. Perhaps leave some of the mould showing, or try adding more slip when the first pouring has set slightly. Splash the inside of a mould, perhaps building up the thickness with different coloured slips.

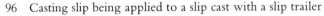

96   Casting slip being applied to a slip cast with a slip trailer

2   Fill a mould with only about half the normal amount of casting slip, leave for a few minutes, then tilt the mould letting the fluid slip run into another part. Continue doing this until all the slip has been absorbed by the mould.

3   Fill a mould with different coloured casting slips. Perhaps add too much oxide so the body blisters, bubbles and fluxes during firings. Trail one colour over the top of another, when the first layer has set or while still wet causing them to intermingle and flow together. Add dry oxide to a casting slip to produce an uneven dispersal of colour.

4   Press leather hard scraps or scrapings of dried casting slip or other clays into the mould before or after pouring in the casting slip.

5   With a two or more piece mould, try wedging pieces of thin clay or cardboard between the pieces of the mould, before pouring in the slip. Do not leave too much of a gap or the casting slip will escape. When the pieces of the mould are separated, the seams on the cast will be thicker and more prominent. These fin-like forms or projections can be carved, pierced, cut, bent or broken. See figures 97a and b.

6   Lay pieces of paper that have been cut or torn, wallpaper or similarly textured material, thin sheets of clay, string or cord, or pieces of fabric or wool in a mould before pouring in the casting slip.

7   Try mixing lengths of string or wool with casting slip before pouring it into a mould. Either pull them out when the cast has set slightly or leave them to burn away in the firing.

Many of the cast forms produced in this way are very fragile, liable to distort or crack in drying, handling or firing. However, the enormous expressive potential is well worth the failure rate. They can also give lively spontaneous qualities when combined with traditionally made casts.

Before being bisque fired slip casts can be modified in much the same way as press moulded forms. Refer back to pages 48 and 49 for suggestions and ways in which they can be developed.

97   a   A two piece mould of a cylinder with pieces held apart with coins
      b   Casts from the mould showing one side of each that has been carved

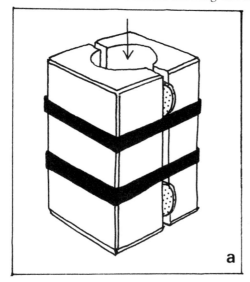
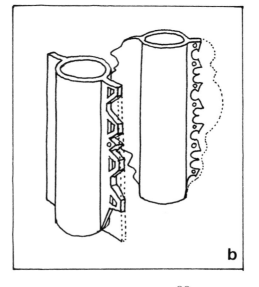

a

b

98 to 100 Pauline Ladd, student

100

101   Judith Mellor, student

102   Judith Mellor, student

103   Jim Johnson, student

104 Marjorie Herbert, student

105 to 107   Pauline Ladd, student

106

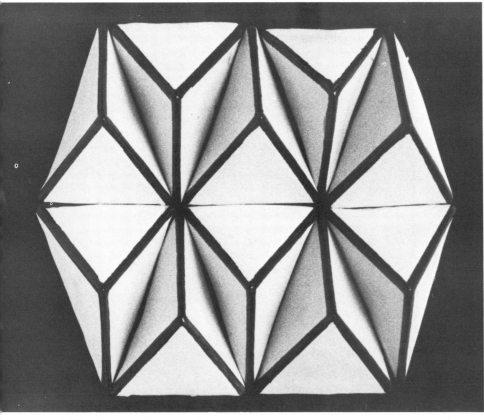

108   Margaret James, student

109   Angela Elwell, aged 14, Eltham Green School

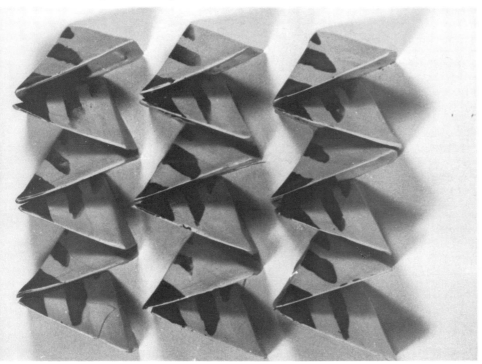

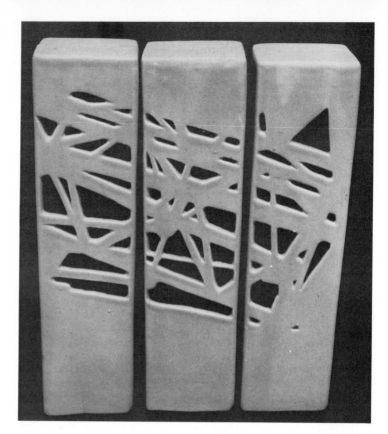

110 and 111   Vivienne Waters, student

112 Vivienne Waters, student

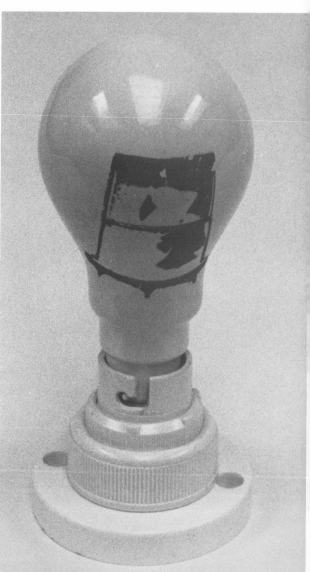

113 and 114   Jim Johnson, student

115   Caroline Reynolds, student

116   Marjorie Herbert, student

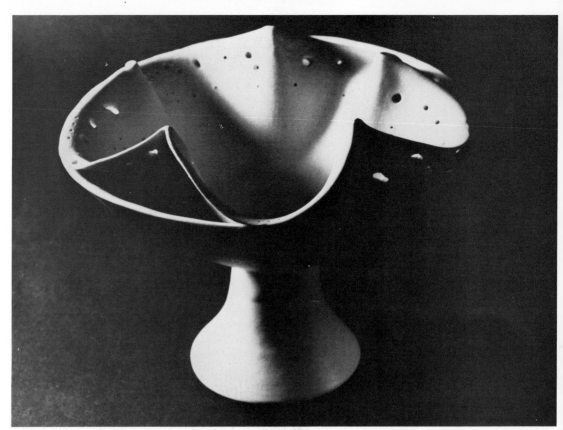

117 to 120   Jan Jackman, student

112

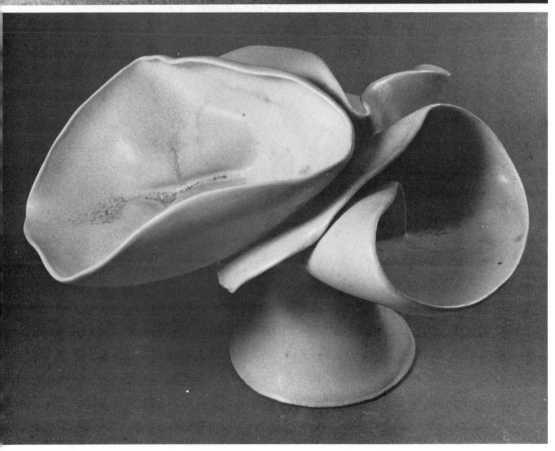

121   Denise Lambert, student

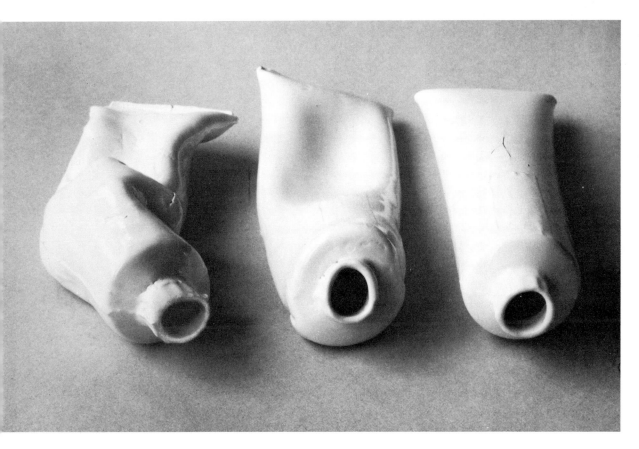

122 and 123   Denise Lambert, student

124 Martha Vaughan, student Barry Summer School

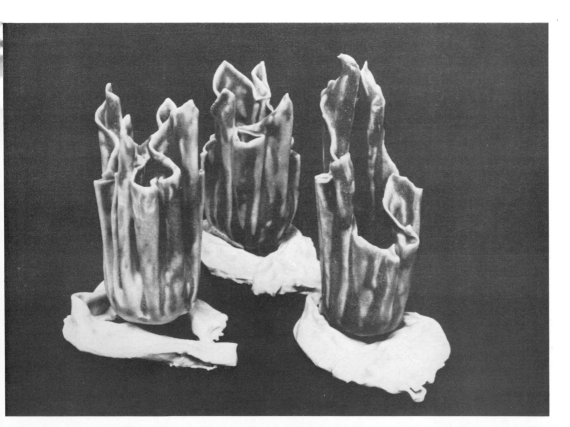

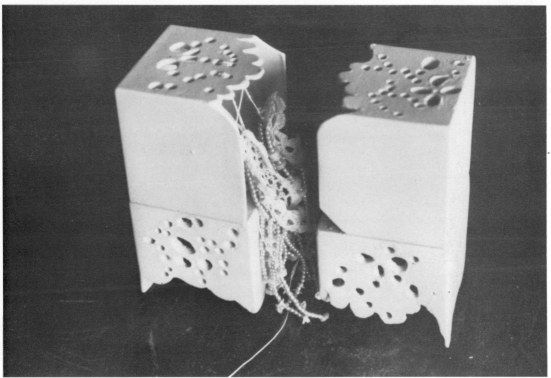

125 Julie Green, student

126 Construction of cut and pierced slip cast porcelain cubes, beads and fibres.
Gladys Hollowood, student Barry Summer School

CONCLUSION

The creative artist working in clay today has a vast range of technical resources and possibilities available to him. This combined with great expressive freedom can create immense problems. The solution for some people working in clay seems to be that of withdrawing to traditional well-established craft standards, ideals and prejudices, rather than attempting to exploit all the available resources and freedom. They seem to be excessively interested and involved in types of processes, rather than the final expressive content of their work. This is clearly shown by the great emphasis on 'technical criticism' in clay work, rather than the more expressive and content orientated criticism in the other arts. With this great interest in technicalities has come the idea that certain processes are inhibiting. One often hears statements like 'The vitality of the spontaneously executed piece, and the indifference of the mould produced one' and 'Moulding processes are only fit for industrial mass production and have little to offer in terms of real contribution to creativity in ceramics'. These are by no means extreme or isolated examples of an attitude against the use of moulds. There has been created a 'hierarchy of processes', which seems to be based on the property of plasticity and it seems that this property must be utilized to the full for a ceramic piece to have quality. Linked with this is the feeling that by adapting industrial processes the individual creative artist would necessarily produce objects similar to those that we would expect from the worst, ill-designed, mass-produced article.

Fortunately, these prejudices are slowly being eroded by some people working in clay that have the imagination and the will to utilize and exploit any process, any material, any tool or equipment, or any deviation from set rules or formulae, if the expressive content of their work is enhanced by it. These attitudes have been taken for granted in other areas of the arts for some time, but only quite recently are they gaining acceptance by people working in clay in this country. For the reader that finds himself involved in any depth in the work suggested in this book, it would be invaluable to spend some time studying the creative use of press moulded and slip casting processes in the work of Paul Astbury, Gordon Baldwin, Glenys Barton, Graham Burr, Mo Jupp, Anthony Hepburn, Gillian Lowndes, Jacqueline Poncelet and Geoffrey Swindell, in this country.

Because the initiation of ideas and their development is so personal a process the following suggestions are only to be taken as guide lines and not rigid rules or stereotypes, but as an encouragement for personal investigations and study. There are no short cuts, or agreed rules, or generally applicable or agreed procedures for developing creative ideas. However, here are some suggestions that may act as incentives to some readers.

It is possible to help yourself by the detailed study and careful observation of the structure, spirit and logic of natural objects, from the tiniest seed pod to vast land forms; man-made objects in a variety of

118

media from the smallest electrical or mechanical component to vast urban landscapes; and the ceramics of all types, cultures and periods. The nature of these investigations should be of slowly attempting to understand and absorb the fundamental principles that determine the variety and particularities of shape, surface, structure and colour in the objects being studied. These should be used as points of departure for personal thought and actions. Remember also that the senseless imitation or copying of objects will provide no long term solution or valuable foundation. Investigations may also be directed towards the 'inner' world of dreams, fantasy, imagination, and all the other manifestations of subconscious levels of thought and insight.

Investigations can also take the form of not visualizing the end result or product, having no preconception or image of what you are trying to achieve. Start with a unit, element, or material, or a combination of two or more of these. Try to combine elements that are new to you. Make slight then drastic changes with each new combination. Move through successive stages, making changes in size and shape, changes in amounts and so on. Start simply then work towards more complex structures and then backwards and forwards between simplicity and complexity. Work systematically, recording, making notes and observations as you go. Above all, train yourself to be aware of the slightest changes and variations that can occur. Be constantly alert, receptive, thoughtful and questioning. Remember, whatever you use, however you start, whatever the basis of your work, it is the expression of your personal attitudes, insights, ideas and feelings in three dimensional terms that should be your main objective.

This book attempts to encourage readers to explore and experiment, while I hope giving them a basic introduction and foundation and some guidelines on technical procedures so that they can provide for themselves a sound basis for the work they attempt. The emphasis is on the development of personal ideas linked with technical processes, rather than just the development of technical expertise for its own sake. The experimentation that is encouraged is not the senseless using of new techniques and new materials, or the superficial searchings for novelty, without there being problems to solve, but the search for a better solution in clay for a personal idea. Linked with this experimental searching must be some discipline. Not that which involves the endless repetition of certain tasks until greater technical proficiency or external standards are achieved but the discipline of methodical analysis, sustained work, enjoyment and concentration; care for materials, equipment and tools; the self-discipline of not being satisfied with less than your best at a particular moment and the discipline of trying to understand a problem and coming to terms with it.

SUPPLIERS

Potterycrafts Ltd
    Campbell Road, Stoke-on-Trent, Staffordshire, ST4 4ET
Potclays Ltd
    Albion Works, Etruria, Stoke-on-Trent, Staffordshire, ST4 7BP
The Fulham Pottery
    210 New Kings Road, London SW6 4NY

BIBLIOGRAPHY

Plaster Mold and Model Making   C. CHANEY AND S. SKEE   Van
    Nostrand Reinhold, New York
Working with Clay and Plaster   DAVID COWLEY   Batsford, London:
    Watson-Guptill, New York
The Technique of Pottery   DORA BILLINGTON AND JOHN COLBECK
    Batsford, London: Watson-Guptill, New York
Clay and Glazes for the Potter   D. RHODES   Chilton, New York
A Potters Book   BERNARD LEACH   Faber, London
The World of the Makers   E. LUCIE-SMITH   Paddington Press
New Ceramics   E. LEWENSTEIN AND E. COOPER   Studio Vista,
    London
Art of the Modern Potter   ANTHONY BIRKS   Country Life, London
Potters on Pottery   E. CAMERON AND P. LEWIS   Evans, London
Objects USA   L. NORDNESS   Thames and Hudson, London
Pottery: Technique of Decoration   JOHN COLBECK   Batsford, London
World Ceramics   R. G. CHARLESTON   Paul Hamlyn, London

MAGAZINES

Ceramics Monthly
American Ceramics
Crafts
American Craft
Ceramic Review